UCHICAGO Consortium on School Research

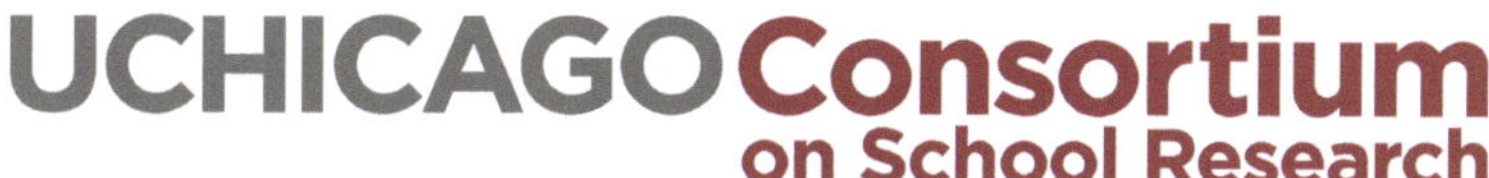

RESEARCH SYNTHESIS OCTOBER 2018

Supporting Social, Emotional, & Academic Development

Research Implications for Educators

Elaine M. Allensworth, Camille A. Farrington, Molly F. Gordon, David W. Johnson, Kylie Klein, Bronwyn McDaniel, and Jenny Nagaoka

TABLE OF CONTENTS

ACKNOWLEDGEMENTS

The authors thank members of UChicago Consortium's research review group, particularly, Penny B. Sebring and Jess Tansey, and our external readers, Bill Kennedy, Kay Fujiyoshi, Dom McCoy, Liam Bird, and Cynthia Nambo, for their helpful feedback. We also thank the UChicago Consortium's communications team, including Jessica Puller and Alida Mitau, as well as freelancer Katelyn Silva, for their work editing and producing this report.

We gratefully acknowledge the W. Clement & Jessie V. Stone Foundation for their support of this work. The UChicago Consortium is also grateful for the support of the Spencer Foundation and the Lewis-Sebring Family Foundation, whose operating grants support the work of the UChicago Consortium, and also appreciates the support from the Consortium Investor Council that funds critical work beyond the initial research: putting the research to work, refreshing the data archive, seeding new studies, and replicating previous studies. Members include: Brinson Foundation, Chicago Community Trust, CME Group Foundation, Crown Family Philanthropies, Lloyd A. Fry Foundation, Joyce Foundation, Lewis- Sebring Family Foundation, McDougal Family Foundation, Osa Foundation, Polk Bros. Foundation, Robert McCormick Foundation, Spencer Foundation, Steans Family Foundation, and The Chicago Public Education Fund.

Cite as: Allensworth, E.M., Farrington, C.A., Gordon, M.F., Johnson, D.W., Klein, K., McDaniel, B., & Nagaoka, J. (2018). *Supporting social, emotional, & academic development: Research implications for educators*. Chicago, IL: University of Chicago Consortium on School Research.

This report was produced by the UChicago Consortium's publications and communications staff: Bronwyn McDaniel, Director of Outreach and Communication; Jessica Puller, Communications Specialist; and Alida Mitau, Development and Communications Coordinator.

Graphic Design: Jeff Hall Design
Photography: Eileen Ryan
Editing: Alida Mitau, Jessica Puller, and Katelyn Silva

10.2018/250/jh.design@rcn.com

Introduction

Over the last decade, dramatic changes have taken place in the education sector that have tremendous potential for improving outcomes for all students—and for changing the profession of teaching. Significant advances in our understanding of how children's brains grow and develop have propelled our growing appreciation of the critical role that social-emotional skills play in learning. There is also increasing recognition of the importance of students' identity development, agency, and socially-valued competencies, along with their academic skills, for long-term success.

A dual focus on the content and rigor of instruction, as well as the social-emotional aspects of learning, has long been recognized as essential in early childhood education and in primary elementary grades. Now, educators from pre-k through high school recognize that focusing only on the content of instruction and students' tested achievement is insufficient to improve educational outcomes and address issues of equity. Concurrently, schools are trying to prepare students for jobs that did not exist a decade ago, and the demands of the modern workforce require new sets of skills and capabilities that emphasize creative problem-solving and teamwork. If young people are to develop these socially valued competencies, they need to play a much more active role in their own learning and have access to opportunities to exercise agency and develop leadership skills.

In this synthesis, we outline the skills and practices that research shows are critical for teachers and principals to best support student success.

Elementary and high school education is evolving from a system designed to "deliver instruction" as it prepares a subset of students for college, to one responsible for identifying and unlocking the potential of all students to succeed in work and life. Today's schools are centered at the nexus of all of these developments, and as a consequence, the profession of education has become far more complicated than it has historically been. Collectively, these shifts are contributing to a moment of opportunity for pre-k–12 teaching practices, and for how schools are organized, to better support the success of all students.

In this research synthesis, we suggest ways that educators can utilize insights from research to create responsive, engaging schools and classrooms that advance educational equity. We define equity in two ways. First, we see equitable schools and classrooms as places that enable everyone to participate fully in learning. This means that learning environments are designed to be developmentally appropriate and responsive to the needs, assets, and cultures of the specific children who inhabit them, and that educators ensure that each child is afforded the necessary opportunities to thrive. Educators and school designers therefore need a solid foundation in learning and development, and the knowledge and skill to support diverse learners. By understanding students' behaviors from a developmental lens (rather than, for example, from a disciplinary lens), educators can respond in ways that support their students' positive growth and holistic development as they improve their classroom culture. Second, equity refers to ultimate results. Education policy increasingly emphasizes the need to identify, understand, and reduce disparities in student performance across lines of race and opportunity, with the goal of achieving equitable outcomes for all students.

Preparing students to meet these new and challenging expectations has led to a shift in what we consider the role of schools and the job of teachers, which in turn requires considerable change in teacher and principal practice. Teachers' responsibilities have gone from managing students through a prescribed curriculum at a set pace, to creating the conditions and building the relationships that can nurture each student's social, emotional, and academic development. Doing this successfully requires significant shifts in how teachers approach their students and their classrooms. The role of the teacher is evolving to be more akin to that of a coach and facilitator than a "sage on the stage." To be successful, educators need opportunities to reflect critically on their own personal and professional experiences, their classroom practices, and the needs of all of their students. This requires support from school leadership and from fellow teachers; it is extremely difficult to change traditional practices without a community of support and a reorganization of how schools are structured. The role of the principal has also evolved from building manager to instructional leader to the architect of collaboration across the school community.

The current momentum in pre-k–12 around social-emotional development and equity presents a critical opportunity to better support students. Since 1990, the University of Chicago Consortium on School Research (UChicago Consortium) has conducted research in partnership with Chicago Public Schools (CPS) to understand what makes schools effective, from which we have gained a high-level perspective on practices that research indicates are most effective for supporting the learning and development of children and adolescents. In this synthesis, we outline the skills and practices that research shows are critical for teachers and principals to best support student success. We hope this brief will help illuminate practices that have significant potential to support teachers and school leaders in meeting the new demands of their work and accelerate and improve outcomes for all students.

The synthesis begins with evidence about student engagement, which is the basis for all learning. The next chapter shows that classroom conditions influence student engagement and begins to make the connection between social-emotional components of learning and classroom structures. The following chapter goes into more detail about students' experiences of the class—how their perceptions and interpretations of themselves in relation to their learning environment influence their engagement, with implications for how teachers can promote encouraging mindsets. Subsequent chapters discuss the value of responsive classrooms, and the importance of family engagement, and what these each mean for school leaders.

CHAPTER 1

Engaging Students in Learning is an Educators' Most Critical Task

It is essential that all students fully participate in learning to reach goals around equity. This may sound obvious, but policymakers and educators often spend a great deal of effort trying to improve student achievement by changing what is taught—changing standards, curriculum, graduation requirements, accountability tests—and less time working to get students more engaged in whatever is taught. Curriculum, standards, and tests don't matter if students are not participating in class and investing themselves in the learning opportunities that teachers prepare.[1]

Engagement has behavioral, emotional, and cognitive components.[2] Behavioral engagement is the degree to which students are doing academic work—attending class, completing assignments, processing material with peers. Students learn by actively working with material, and it is that process of grappling that allows new skills and content to stick.[3] Student engagement also includes emotional components that have to do with a student's interest in, enjoyment of, or anxiety about course material, as well as feelings about teachers, peers, or school as a whole. The degree to which students feel interested and connected is consequential to their learning and future engagement. Human brains cannot maintain focus on things we find to be boring, even with extensive effort, and feeling anxious, threatened, or unwelcome interferes with cognitive functioning. The more students are emotionally engaged in school, the more easily they can focus their attention and direct their behavior toward learning.[4] Cognitive engagement is the degree to which students are actively focused on learning, not just going through the motions, but working to master new

skills or knowledge.[5] In practice, all of these are interrelated. Only behavioral engagement is observable by others, making it a crucial signal of overall engagement to which educators need to attend.

Why Talk About Student Engagement? Everyone Already Knows It Matters

Many students show weak engagement in school.
The most basic requirement to be engaged in learning is to be present. Yet, nationally, about 15 percent of K–12 students—almost 20 percent of high school students, and more than 10 percent of elementary school students—are chronically absent, missing at last 10 percent of class time.[6] There will continue to be large disparities in educational outcomes, with many students struggling in school, as long as one-fifth of high school students and one-tenth of elementary students are chronically missing considerable amounts of school.

---

1 Curricular and testing reforms often have no positive effects and can even have negative effects. For example, simply requiring college-preparatory coursework, or enrolling academically strong students in early algebra, or focusing on preparation for the ACT were not found to benefit student achievement (Allensworth, Nomi, Montgomery, & Lee, 2009; Montgomery, Allensworth, & Correa, 2010; Clotfelter, Ladd, & Vigdor, 2015).

2 Fredricks, Blumenfeld, & Paris (2004); Appleton, Christenson, & Furlong (2008).

3 Bransford, Brown, & Cocking (1999).

4 Mahatmya, Lohman, Matjasko, & Farb (2018); Steele (1997).

5 Fredericks et al. (2004).

6 U.S. Department of Education (2018); Chang, Bauer, & Byrnes (2018).

If students are in class, then they are able to put in effort. Through repetition, practice, and application of course material, they expand and differentiate the neural pathways in their brains, allowing new information and skills to stick. While children are relatively engaged in school when they are younger, they become less motivated and less academically engaged as they move from elementary school to middle school to high school.[7] This mirrors the increase in absenteeism that occurs as students enter the middle grades, which further accelerates in high school.

Disengagement cuts across racial/ethnic, socioeconomic, and achievement lines. Yet, the consequences of disengagement are more significant for students from families with fewer resources; there are more second chances and supports outside of school for students from more affluent families.[8] Even in high-achieving schools, where students are working hard, emotional disengagement can lead to stress, cheating, and lower well-being than students who are fully engaged in their learning. Studies have consistently found that about one-half of the students in high school are bored and disengaged.[9] When students feel disinterested in a subject, it requires extra energy to pay attention—causing mental fatigue and a cognitive inability to focus, which in turn can further undermine students' feelings about and connections to school.[10] For teachers, student disengagement fosters classroom management challenges, often leading to teacher burnout.[11]

Teachers are more often encouraged to focus on "what" is being learned rather than to grapple with why students are not fully participating in the process of learning. Lesson planning, content coverage, and test preparation can take all of educators' time, leaving little time to reflect on why it is that not all students are fully engaged in the work that has been asked of them. Taking the time to figure out why students are falling behind and devising strategies to help them catch up can even seem contradictory to teachers' roles as evaluators of student performance. It can seem like lesson planning is the work of the teacher, while it is up to students to put in the effort to learn. But if educators simply assign low grades without finding out why students are not fully participating, then they are not having success with those students.

A focus on student engagement requires a change in priorities from not only identifying how well students are meeting expectations, to also working to get all students able to meet those expectations. There are myriad reasons students might miss class or not do the work that their teacher asks of them, and those reasons could stem from issues outside of the classroom, or inside of it, and often comes from a combination of both. It takes considerable reflection, and strong skills and practices, for teachers to be able to engage all students around challenging work. The more that teachers are working with students who have not been academically successful in the past, the more difficult this is to do. School is a system that generally motivates students who already have a track record of academic success, who have strong supports for learning at home, and/or who can readily see the connection between their efforts in the classroom and their future opportunities. As a result, there usually is stronger student participation and less disruption in classes with more high-achieving students and fewer low-achieving students.[12] But, this is a function of the system, not of the young people in schools. Meeting goals around equity, and getting all students ready to succeed in college, requires teachers and school leaders to identify and provide what it is that students need to fully engage in their learning so that it is not just a subset of students who are successful. This means that teaching is a harder job in some schools and classrooms than in others.

---

7   Eccles, Wigfield, & Schiefele (1998); Marks (2000); National Research Council (2004); Stipek (2002).

8   National Research Council (2004)

9   Marks (2000); Steinberg, Brown, & Dornbush (1996).

10 Farrington (2014); Kaplan & Kaplan (1982).

11 Brouwers & Tomic (2000).

12 Jiang & Sporte (2016); Whitehurst, Chingos, & Lindquist (2014); Allensworth, Gwynne, Moore, & de la Torre (2014); Nomi & Allensworth (2013); Sebastian, Allensworth, & Stevens (2014).

Isn't Engagement a Low-Level Goal, When We Want Students to Develop High-Level Skills?

If students aren't showing up to class, or putting in effort, they are not engaged in learning and do not have a chance to develop high-level skills. Improving attendance and effort may be a low-level goal, but because these are basic requirements for teaching and learning to occur, they are critically important to attend to; otherwise, nothing else matters. Missing class and assignments are also signals that students are not emotionally or cognitively engaged, or that there are factors keeping them from being able to engage in class. It may seem like a student doesn't care, when she is actually taking care of a sick parent at night, lacks transportation to get to school, or is stressed about conflict with peers. Teachers can promote engagement, improve student outcomes, and improve their own practice, by finding out why students aren't fully participating, and figuring out what it is that their students need.

Attendance and effort are the main drivers of students' course grades, grade point averages (GPAs), course failure, high school graduation, and college readiness—much more so than test scores, demographic factors, or which classes students take.[13] It may seem like it's OK for students to miss class now and then, or to miss an assignment here or there, but it seems OK because nobody sees what would have happened if the student had been in class or finished the assignment. Even just a couple of days of absence or a few missed assignments can cause students to fall behind, and once students fall behind, it becomes increasingly harder to catch up.[14] Often, students and their families don't realize how much school they've missed. Missing just a couple of days a month adds up to almost a month of missed instructional time over the year and makes a student chronically absent. Students who are chronically absent are at high risk of failing classes when they get to high school and, eventually, not graduating.[15] Students who are chronically absent in pre-k and the elementary grades make smaller gains on tests and are likely to score at levels that put them far behind proficiency levels.[16] At the same time, students who have high attendance show higher learning gains than other students, while schools that improve attendance rates show increases in students' test gains, grades, and pass rates.[17]

CONSIDER THESE FACTS:

- Students who earn high school GPAs of 3.0 or better—the grades that indicate readiness for college—tend to have attendance rates (on average) of 98 percent in the middle-grade years. Their test scores in the middle grades are much less predictive of how they do in high school than their grades and attendance in the middle grades.[18]

- Missing just five days of school in the first semester of ninth grade decreases the likelihood of eventually graduating high school by 25 percentage points.[19]

- GPAs decline by almost one-half of a GPA point, on average, when students enter high school, and this decline is almost completely explained by increased absences and weaker study habits compared to students' behaviors in the middle grades.[20] This decline in attendance and effort takes many students off-track for college, even among students with strong achievement in middle school.

High school GPAs, which are largely a reflection of the effort that students put into their classes, are by far the strongest predictors of college graduation.[21] Course grades show who is ready for college much more than test scores. On average, students need to earn a B average or better in high school to have at least a 50

---

13 Allensworth & Luppescu (2018); BERC (2011).

14 Farrington (2014).

15 Allensworth & Easton (2007); Neild & Balfanz (2006); Balfanz, Herzog, & MacIver (2007); Allensworth et al. (2014).

16 Ehrlich, Gwynne, & Allensworth (2018); Ready (2010); Ginsburg, Jordan, & Chang (2014).

17 Balfanz & Byrnes (2013); Allensworth, Healey, Gwynne, & Crespin (2016).

18 Allensworth et al. (2014).

19 Allensworth & Easton (2007).

20 Rosenkranz et al. (2014).

21 Allensworth & Clark (2018); Bowen, Chingos, & McPherson (2009); Geiser & Santelices (2007); Hiss & Franks (2014); Hoffman & Lowitzki (2005); Kobrin, Patterson, Shaw, Mattern, & Barbuti (2008); Rothstein (2004).

percent chance of graduating from college, among those who enroll in a four-year college.[22] This is much more important than reaching any test benchmark, including on the ACT or SAT.

CONSIDER THESE FACTS:

- Students who reach ACT's reading benchmark (21) have a 50 percent chance of getting As or Bs in a college social science class, while students with a much lower score (16) have a 40 percent chance—not much of a difference in college outcomes despite very different scores.[23]

- Among students who have the same ACT scores (21–23) and enroll in a four-year college, college graduation rates are 77 percent among those with a high school GPA of 3.5 or higher, but 40 percent among those with a high school GPA of 2.0–2.4. Earning good grades in high school greatly increases chances of graduating from college among students with the same test scores.[24]

- High grades also have benefits for test scores—test-score gains are strongly related to the grades students receive in their corresponding course.[25]

Why Aren't Students Engaged in School and Earning High Grades?

There are myriad reasons students might not be putting a lot of effort into their coursework. A lack of effort can be interpreted to mean that a student doesn't care about school, or that their families don't care if they succeed. Yet, students and their families usually care a lot about school performance; there are just other factors that influence students' academic behaviors.

Teachers' classroom practices influence student engagement. While student effort is often taken as a signal about the student—whether they care about learning or are academically motivated—it is also a reflection of how educators are showing up for their students. As discussed in the following chapters, the ways that educators structure classes and build relationships with students influence students' feelings and perceptions about themselves, their class, the work, and school. These mindsets, in turn, strongly influence the degree to which students put in effort and persevere at challenging tasks. The ways in which classes are run influence the degree to which factors outside of the classroom interfere with engagement inside of the classroom. Often, there are cultural gaps between teachers and students, which limit teachers' ability to be effective.[26] Culturally responsive teaching, discussed further in subsequent chapters, is an instructional framework in which teachers reflect on their own cultural position and adapt their practice to leverage students' cultural and linguistic resources as assets to build upon, rather than barriers to learning.[27] Engaging all students in learning requires teachers to be reflective about themselves and how their teaching practice is perceived by each of their students.

The design of the school influences student engagement. Students put in more effort and attend class more often under some school conditions more than others. We can see this when we follow students through school transitions—the same student under different conditions will change their academic behaviors. It is very common when students transition from elementary school to middle school, or from middle school to high school, that they start missing class more often, missing assignments, or studying less.[28] Even students with strong test scores can start earning low grades when this happens, and they can get off-track for college or be at jeopardy for not graduating high school.[29] The fact that the same student will engage differently depending on the school and classroom context shows that educators have influence. As discussed in subsequent chapters, school leaders can create structures that facilitate

22 Roderick, Nagaoka, Allensworth, Coca, Correa, & Stoker (2006); Bowen et al. (2009).

23 Based on a graph of the relationship between ACT scores and grades at a "typical" college in Allen & Sconing (2005).

24 Healey, Nagaoka, & Michelman (2014).

25 Allensworth, Correa, & Ponisciak (2008); Easton, Johnson, & Sartain (2017).

26 Gay (2010); Ladson-Billings (2009).

27 Aceves & Orosco (2014); Villegas & Luca (Mar. 2007).

28 Rosenkranz et al. (2014); Alspaugh (1998); Eccles, Lord, & Midgley (1991).

29 Allensworth & Easton (2005); Allensworth et al. (2014) *Absenteeism from Preschool to High School*, available at https://consortium.uchicago.edu/page/presentations

teacher collaboration around supporting students and promoting a climate that supports engagement across the school.

Family resources influence engagement. All families with children know that it takes a lot of resources to support students through school—time, money, and parents' own education and knowledge about school. It takes reliable transportation, quiet places to study, and adults who are able to help students navigate through struggles that will inevitably occur at school. Many of the causes of absenteeism and lack of effort around schoolwork are associated with different levels of access to resources—children's and family health and access to health care, resources for transportation and basic needs, competing responsibilities at home, or commitments with peers.[30] These influencers are often invisible to teachers and administrators, unless they talk with students and their families.

Improving student engagement in school requires educators to be constantly reflective about their own practice, and how they are influencing student engagement. There are many factors that influence student engagement, and much that educators can do to improve it. Doing so requires much more of educators than a traditional framework that accepts that some students will simply be checked out from learning. There is substantial work to be done to make sure all students are fully engaged, and for educators to have the resources, skills, and supports they need to be able to fully engage all students in all classrooms. While challenging, this work is essential to reach goals of equitable outcomes for students.

---

30 Allensworth et al. (2014) *Absenteeism from Preschool to High School,* available at https://consortium.uchicago.edu/page/presentations

CHAPTER 2

Classroom Conditions and Teacher Practices Influence Engagement

Academic development inherently has social-emotional components. When humans work hard to learn something, it is because they want to have a particular feeling or avoid a particular feeling. Students put the effort into learning because they feel connected to the material, they want to make parents or their teacher proud, they want to feel competent, or they want to avoid humiliation or feeling left out.[31]

In early childhood, social-emotional development is seen as a critical part of learning, but it is often overlooked in older grades. High-quality pre-k programs strive to develop students' social skills and executive functioning (working memory, self-control, and attentional skills) as a critical part of early learning. Intentional efforts to develop students' attention and social-emotional skills can be effective for improving their social relationships and their academic performance, which then serve as the building blocks for further learning.[32]

> Academic development inherently has social-emotional components.

In the early elementary grades, teachers usually still think of themselves as "teachers of children" and not just teachers of academic content. However, the emphasis on social-emotional development often dissipates as students move into higher grade-levels and teachers increasingly focus on course content. Beginning in third grade, educators are often under pressure to raise test scores, and this can lead them to engage in counterproductive practices for student learning and development. In fact, the more that there's a focus on just test scores, the less there is a focus on better practices that really help students learn.[33] Upper-elementary and middle-grades teachers often struggle to find the time and space to focus on "the whole child" amid test-based accountability demands on their practice.

In high school, course content becomes a primary concern, as educators use coursework to prepare students for college and the workforce. High school educators may leave students' social-emotional development to families or after-school programs, while teachers focus on "academics." As a result, opportunities for young people to develop social-emotional skills, productive mindsets, and healthy adult identities are often inequitably distributed. Students with fewer financial resources or competing economic or family demands are less likely to have access to, or participate in, after-school programs, summer internships, study-abroad experiences, or other youth development opportunities that benefit their more advantaged peers. The multifaceted peer environment of a high school classroom is an ideal place to develop the habits, mindsets, and interpersonal skills that will serve a young person well throughout life, but these social-emotional competencies can be neglected when the main focus is on course content. Ironically, recognition of the need for strong social and emotional skills resurfaces when students leave school and enter the workforce. A 2018 poll of business executives and hiring managers found that the skills they most valued in recent college graduates included being able to work effectively in teams, having ethical judgment and decision-making, being able to work independently, and being self-motivated.[34]

Executive function and social skills continue to develop throughout childhood and adolescence, and influence students' behavior and engagement in the classroom. Developing "whole children" means that teachers pay attention to social-skills training as an integral part of supporting their students' learning and development—and as an important way to build a

---

31 Dawes & Larson (2011); Immordino-Yang (2016).
32 Center on the Developing Child at Harvard University (2011).
33 Allensworth et al. (2008); Koretz (2017); Nagaoka et al. (2015).
34 Hart Research Associates (2018).

productive classroom community. Paying attention to students' social-emotional development is not a substitution for teaching academic content, it is a change in how academic content is taught. The ways that teachers set up their classes influence students' emotional connection to their school work and their interactions with their teacher and peers. These, in turn, influence students' engagement and learning. By incorporating routines into their academic lessons that support student collaboration and connections to the subjects they are studying, teachers can not only promote social-emotional development, but also deepen students' content-area knowledge and skills.[35]

Students Change Their Level of Effort in Different Class Contexts

The same student can get very different grades as they take different courses, change grade levels, and go to different schools. Students may generally get high grades or low ones, but most students get different grades in different courses, and they can show improvements or declines in their course grades over time, especially when they enter new schools. These changes are largely due to differences in their attendance and study habits as they enter different contexts—students put more effort into their schoolwork under some conditions than others.[36] Providing opportunities for teachers to engage each other around data on how the same students perform in different classrooms can give teachers insight on how their practices may be affecting student engagement. The ways that teachers structure their classes can encourage or discourage strong participation and learning—and what works for some students might not work for others.[37]

Students show the highest learning gains in classes that are not only challenging, but also where students are actually doing the work that aligns with their teachers' expectations.[38] These are not necessarily "quiet" classrooms, but classrooms where students focus on work that challenges them. It is not sufficient for teach-

ers to introduce challenging work if students are not doing that work, or for students to be working hard on work that is not challenging. As discussed below, the more that work is challenging, the harder it can be to get students to put in the effort needed to be successful.

Student-centered practices, where students are actively working during class on interactive lessons, are most effective for learning. It is the process of productive struggle that develops the neural pathways that allow new skills and information to stick. Educators can offer a challenging curriculum that is teacher-centered—where the teacher lectures on difficult and new topics to students, but students can only learn so much by sitting and listening. Teachers can make a class challenging by asking students to do a large quantity of work, but only those students who actually do the work will grow from the experience, and teachers risk turning off other students from the tedium of long assignments that do not hold their interest.

> The most equitable classrooms use student-centered instructional practices and create the conditions that allow each student to be highly engaged. Learning comes about through cycles of action and reflection—where students encounter, tinker, choose, practice, and contribute to new experiences, and then describe, evaluate, connect, envision, and integrate to make meaning of those experiences.[39]

To be successful at challenging new tasks, students need guidance from adults and more experienced peers who can demonstrate what to do and provide models of what success looks like. Also, students may need to explicitly be taught new learning strategies and supported to develop new study habits to be able to handle challenging expectations, and these may need to be modeled by the teacher as part of the learning process.[40]

35 Bransford et al. (2000); National Research Council and the Institute of Medicine (2004).
36 Allensworth & Luppescu (2018); Rosenkranz et al. (2014).
37 Farrington et al. (2012).

38 Allensworth, Gwynne, Pareja, Sebastian, & Stevens (2014); Kane & Cantrell (2010).
39 Nagaoka et al. (2015).
40 Farrington et al. (2012); Nagaoka et al. (2015).

 Students need new concepts to link in some way to things they already know, or they will not have the mental maps that their brains need to process the material.[41] Students learn the most when the work that is asked of them is challenging, but not so challenging that they have little chance of success. Besides being aware of students' skill levels, teachers need to reflect on how relevant and connected the material is to students of differing cultural backgrounds. Culturally responsive teaching practices build off of students' personal experiences and interests, engaging students through interactive and collaborative practices.[42]

Students and teachers need more support when work becomes more challenging. Policymakers will often put in place new standards, tests, or curricula, without guidance about how to implement them. The fact is, when students are asked to do very challenging work, they can get frustrated. Hard work is hard by definition. Introducing more challenging work without sufficient supports or attention to students' emotions and learning strategies to handle the more difficult work can lead to student frustration, withdrawal, and disruption. Students can end up learning less than when they were exposed to less challenging work.[43] Thus, teachers can be hesitant to change practices, for fear that students will disengage. Or, they revert to traditional ways of teaching when unable to get students to do the more challenging work.

Students get higher grades in classes where teachers provide strong support for learning, regardless of the level of challenge. Academic challenge is essential for learning but raising the level of challenge in a class without changing the amount of support students receive makes them more likely to fail and receive low grades.[44] Even high-achieving students get lower grades and can become at risk of failure in their most difficult classes.[45] However, in classrooms where students report high levels of teacher support, grades are above average regardless of how challenging the classes are. In fact, grades are higher in challenging classrooms with high levels of support than in classrooms where the work is easier, but the teacher provides little support.[46] Coupling challenging work with high expectations and high levels of support is the best way for teachers to promote student learning and academic success.

As discussed in Chapter 3, support comes from clear explanations, monitoring how students are doing, giving clear instructions, and reaching out when students need help. The more that students feel they can succeed—that they have self-efficacy—the more likely they are to put in effort, even when the work is hard. Interviews with students show that they value those teachers who help them succeed in their classes and reach their larger educational goals.[47] When teachers intentionally design their class so that all students can succeed, students come to trust their teachers and are more willing to put in the effort needed to learn.

---

41 Bransford et al. (2000).
42 Aceves & Orosco (2014).
43 Sporte, Hart, & Wechsler (2009); Allensworth et al. (2009).
44 Allensworth et al. (2014).
45 Nomi & Allensworth (2009); Allensworth & Luppescu (2018).
46 Allensworth et al. (2014).
47 Rosenkranz et al. (2014).

CHAPTER 3

Teachers Shape Students' Mindsets, Changing Their Learning Experience

The research on classroom climate and teacher instructional support demonstrates that teachers have tremendous power to influence student engagement and learning. Importantly, teachers' power resides in *how* they set up learning experiences for their students and the kinds of interactions students and teachers have together in the classroom. As every educator knows, learning requires focused attention and effort on the part of the learner. Students cannot develop the content knowledge and skills necessary to become fluent thinkers and problem-solvers unless they feel motivated to do so. In the past, many teachers assumed that motivation was something students had to bring with them to class. Students who were motivated could learn, and the ones whom the teacher perceived as being unmotivated—well, there was nothing the teacher could do for them. Some of the most exciting research from the science of learning and development points to how students' perceptions of the classroom and desire to engage in learning are shaped by how their learning experience is organized. The findings help teachers understand the conditions that *activate* students' intrinsic motivation—the kind of motivation that deepens young people's engagement and persistence in academic tasks, improves the quality of the work they produce, and increases their overall enjoyment of learning.

Teachers can deepen student motivation and improve academic performance by changing students' psychological experiences in the classroom. Human beings are wired to seek out places and situations where they feel connected to other people, where they are able to engage in meaningful activities, and where they feel like their efforts will lead to success.[48] Whether or not students *experience* these conditions during each school day and what they *believe* about their own potential for success has a strong influence on their willingness to put effort into learning. Researchers use the term "academic mindsets" or "learning mindsets" to refer to students' perceptions of a learning setting and their beliefs about themselves and their work in that setting.[49] While students' experiences and beliefs are certainly shaped by family, peers, and the media, it is becoming clear that teachers and other school staff are in a unique position to change students' daily experiences and beliefs in ways that have real beneficial effects on students' academic performance.[50]

Four learning mindsets are particularly important in supporting students' academic behaviors, persistence, and performance on academic tasks. Expressed from the point of view of a student, the four mindsets are:

- I belong in this learning community.
- I can succeed at this.
- My ability and competence grow with my effort (also known as a "growth mindset").
- This work has value for me.[51]

How *true* these statements feel within a classroom determines how likely students are to focus their attention on learning and persevere with challenging academic tasks. Feeling like any of these is *not* true (for example, feeling like they *don't* belong, or feeling like they *can't* be successful) will make students more likely to disengage from learning. Research has consistently found that students with more positively oriented mindsets engage in better academic behaviors (they have better attendance and are more likely to participate in class, study, and complete homework) and earn better grades than students for whom these belief statements don't feel true.[52]

---

48 Deci & Ryan (2008); Farrington et al. (2012); Halpern, Heckman, & Larson (2013); Maslow (1943); Osher & Kendziora (2010).
49 Farrington et al. (2012); Quay & Romero (2015).
50 Yeager & Walton (2011).
51 Farrington et al. (2012).
52 Farrington et al. (2012).

 Teachers can have a strong
influence on students' mindsets through the messages
they communicate to students and the conditions that
they set for learning. In fact, research has shown that the
same student can have different mindsets from one classroom to the next, and that students earn higher or lower
grades in their different classrooms as their mindsets
change. Further, differences in students' mindsets across
classes can be traced to differences in their teachers'
instructional practices or in the learning conditions that
teachers create in their classrooms.[53] Teachers can cultivate positive student mindsets—or change maladaptive
mindsets—by engaging in instructional practices that
align with students' psychological needs.

It is important for teachers to understand that they
are unlikely to change students' mindsets by trying
to convince students to feel differently about school.
Instead, teachers' real power comes from creating a
different experience for students in their classrooms.

By engaging in instructional practices that align with
students' psychological and academic needs, teachers
create the motivational conditions that directly support
students in putting forth the effort and focus required
to engage in classroom tasks and come to deeply learn
and enjoy academic challenges.

 As young people enter middle school and
high school, they are often preoccupied with themselves
and their peer groups. This is because an adolescent's
primary "task," from a psychological standpoint, is to
develop a healthy identity that can carry them into adulthood. Younger children have simpler notions of identity,
which they tend to think about in fairly concrete terms:
"I am a girl" or "I'm good at soccer" or "I love reading."
Adolescence is the time when students are actively developing a range of social identities beyond their member-
ship in a family. They are newly conscious of and actively
grappling with what it means to be a gendered and racial-

How Can Teachers Develop Students' Positive Academic Mindsets?

Teachers can cultivate positive student mindsets—or change maladaptive mindsets—by engaging in
instructional practices that align with students' psychological needs. These include:

- Setting predictable norms and routines that
support respectful student and teacher
interactions in the classroom;

- Sending clear messages to students about
the nature and purpose of learning and the
role of mistakes in the learning process; [54]

- Explicitly connecting new material to students'
prior knowledge; [55]

- Helping students "see themselves" in the
work by connecting it to their interests,
goals, or cultural identities; [56]

- Developing trust by listening to students and
responding to their input; [57]

- Creating opportunities for student autonomy and
choice as well as for collaborative learning with
their peers; [58]

- Showing students models of high-quality work
and conveying confidence that they can produce
equally good work; [59]

- Providing frequent and specific feedback on
students' work and opportunities for students
to apply that feedback to progressively improve
their performance; [60] and

- Ensuring fair grading practices that emphasize
growth and improvement.[61]

53 Farrington, Porter, & Klugman (forthcoming).
54 Mueller & Dweck (1998).
55 Bransford et al. (2000).
56 Gay (2010).
57 Oldfather & McLaughlin (1993); Roehlkepartain et al. (2017).
58 Deci & Ryan (2008); Ginsburg-Block, Rohrbeck, & Fantuzzo (2006).
59 Osher & Kendziora (2010).
60 Hattie & Gan (2011).
61 Brookhard (2004).

ized individual in American society. Adolescents have to figure out what prevalent stereotypes about gender, race, and culture actually mean for who they are.[62] All of this comes into the classroom with them. To a large extent, how young people situate themselves in relation to academic learning will be shaped by the ways in which they see academic interest and competence as being aligned or misaligned with their developing social identities: Is school something that "people like me" care about and are good at? How students come to answer this question for themselves is likely to have a strong influence on the level of focus and effort they apply to learning and enjoying academic work.[63]

Teachers who understand child and adolescent development can use that knowledge to design engaging and supportive classrooms. From pre-k through twelfth grade, students have three jobs: learning about the world, learning about others, and learning about themselves. While students at every age are always in the process of learning something about all three of these, there are particular leverage points at particular ages that teachers can use to best support student motivation and learning.

For example, **pre-k and early elementary teachers (grades Pre-K–4)** can feed children's voracious interest in learning about the outside world by exposing them to as many new places, people, and things as possible—and developing the vocabulary to talk about and reflect on their experiences.[64] At the same time, early elementary students need particular support in building their awareness of other people's feelings and developing skills to control their own attention and behaviors.[65]

As students move into **late-elementary and middle grades (grades 5–8),** they tend to become increasingly preoccupied with "the self." They define themselves largely in terms of their connection to particular peer groups and are likely to take on the behaviors, language,

tastes, and interests of their peers.[66] Students at this age can become overly concerned with their appearance or their likeability. This is also a time when children become increasingly aware of different kinds of social power, and adults might see an increase in social cliques as well as bullying behavior. At this age, students who feel estranged from or ostracized by classmates have a very difficult time focusing on learning.[67] In extreme cases, this poses a significant threat to children's mental health and well-being.[68] Middle-grade teachers understand how important it is to their students to feel respected and comfortable, and they work hard to foster a classroom environment that provides psychological and physical safety for everyone.[69]

The **entrance to high school (grades 9–10)** generally corresponds to the entry into early adolescence, when young people actively develop their identities as racialized and gendered people.[70] They are coming to understand what it means to be a Latina or a Black male or a White transgendered person within their immediate families and communities, within their school, and within the larger social world. Students' interests and future aspirations are seen through these new lenses of social identity.[71] Teachers who understand this developmental period will provide students with a wide range of role models within their discipline so that every young person can see a place for themselves in that subject.[72] Teachers create optimal conditions for learning for early adolescents when they actively affirm students' social identities and send a clear message that they see these identities as being consistent with deep intellectual capacity and promise.[73]

As students move into the **upper grades of high school (grades 11–12),** they become increasingly focused on questions of meaning and purpose. Juniors and seniors are actively trying to discover or construct what their adult lives might look like, where they "belong" in the world, and what they have to contribute.[74] Teachers

---

62 Aronson (2002); Halpern et al. (2013); Helms (1995); Nagaoka et al. (2015); Oyserman & Fryberg (2006); Phinney & Ong (2007).
63 Murphy & Zerkel (2015); Oyserman (2008); Oyserman & Fryberg (2006).
64 Bodrova, Germeroth, & Leong (2013); Cole, Armstrong, & Pemberton (2010).
65 National Research Council and Institute of Medicine (2000).
66 Gutgesell & Payne (2004); Hazen, Scholzman, & Beresin (2008).
67 Nansel et al. (2001).
68 Kupersmidt & Cole (1990).
69 Yeager, Dahl, & Dweck (2017).
70 Phinney (1993).
71 Oyserman & Fryberg (2006).
72 Zirkel (2002).
73 Immordino-Yang, Darling-Hammond, & Krone (2018); Romero (2015).

can best support their students' engagement by help-ing them make personal connections to their learning and providing opportunities for students to apply their knowledge and skills to solving real-world problems.[75] Grappling with the ethical implications of adult choices (whether considered through the lens of a fictional character, a figure in history, a scientist, or students' own lives) allows adolescents to articulate their own values and develop their "ethical muscles" as they work to apply those values to increasingly complex situations.[76]

Learning is a complex social, emotional, and cogni-tive process embedded within the multifaceted envi-ronment of a classroom. Being able to figure out which interventions work, when, for whom, and under what conditions requires that teachers experiment with dif-ferent approaches and keep open channels of commu-nication with their students to better understand how they are experiencing their learning environment.

 While research can provide direction for teachers as they work toward building more engaging and supportive class-rooms, personal reflection and talking with students are perhaps the two best ways for teachers to grow in their practice. Considering questions such as these can aid teacher reflection:

- What do I do now to create a welcoming and respect-ful culture and climate in my classroom, and how might students participate in developing and rein-forcing positive norms for behavior?

- How do I communicate with students about why I want to give them challenging learning opportunities? How might different students hear those messages?

- What do students find most helpful in the supports I offer now, and what ideas might they have for other kinds of support that would help them with challenging work?

- How might school or classroom policies reinforce stereotypes or inadvertently send negative messages to some of my students about their opportunities for success—and how might I change that?

 As we saw in the previous chapters, student engagement really matters for students' learning and long-term outcomes. Over time, positive mindsets and active engagement in learning not only support deeper understanding and better academic achievement, but they also tend to increase students' enjoyment of learning and develop-ment of positive academic identities. When students see themselves as learners, they are more likely to choose to enroll in more rigorous courses, complete high school, and go on to college.[77] Conversely, maladaptive mindsets become part of a negative cycle: students withdraw from learning, leading to gaps in their academic understanding that further undermine their confidence, enjoyment, and future learning. Students for whom any of the four learning mindsets don't ring true are more likely to want to avoid future academic situations and refrain from taking advanced academic classes if they have a choice. Teachers can pay attention to students' comments or behaviors that might indicate maladaptive mindsets: feelings that students don't belong or don't see themselves as being able to succeed in the classroom, beliefs that they aren't smart enough to figure out challenging problems, or perceptions that work is meaningless or irrelevant to their lives or futures. Talking with students one-on-one about their experiences in school can provide teachers with insights about how changing some aspects of their classroom or instructional practice might also change students' experience and level of engagement.

---

74 Halpern, Heckman, & Larson (2013); Immordino-Yang, Darling-Hammond, & Krone (2018); Yeager & Bundick (2009).
75 Darling-Hammond et al. (forthcoming); Halpern, Heckman, & Larson (2013).
76 Halstead & Taylor (2000); Vincent (2001).
77 Farrington et al. (2012); Nasir, McLaughlin, & Jones (2009).

CHAPTER 4

Responsive Classrooms Enable All Students to Engage

While teachers and classrooms directly shape children's motivation and engagement in school in profound ways, experiences outside school also affect how students experience their classrooms and schools in important ways. Teachers' efforts to create classroom environments that are responsive to students' individual social and emotional needs can enable all students, but particularly those who have experienced significant trauma outside of school, to engage fully and succeed. Each year, millions of students experience significant trauma, such as the death or chronic illness of a loved one, family conflict or separation, extreme damage to home or property, homelessness, food insecurity, neglect or abuse, sexual assault, or exposure to community violence. While all students are at some risk for experiencing traumatic events, poverty creates a much higher likelihood, and an ongoing history of racial oppression in the United States places low income children of color at substantially higher risk of experiencing an array of adverse or traumatic events.[78] Thus, helping teachers understand and respond to the ways that traumatic stresses may shape how students experience their classrooms and schools is critical to creating more equitable learning environments such that all children have the opportunity to participate fully and succeed.

Traumatic stress—and chronic traumatic stress, in particular—may directly and negatively affect student's performance in school. The more exposure students have to adverse, stressful experiences—and the more severe those experiences—the greater the chances they will struggle academically in schools.[79] Children's exposure to homicides in the communities where they

Educators' critical self-awareness and appreciation of how traumatic stress may affect children's experience of their classrooms are key to responding in supportive ways that enable all children to participate fully and succeed.

live, for example, is associated with both impaired attention and impulse control,[80] as well as poorer performance on IQ tests[81] and standardized achievement tests,[82] including assessments of both reading[83] and math.[84] Children's exposure to community violence is also associated with lower attendance.[85] The negative effects of children's traumatic experiences may have far-reaching implications both for children and schools. Children's access to magnet and selective schooling options and programs, as well as college choices, are often at least partially determined by standardized test scores. Likewise, schools, whose ratings under district accountability policies may similarly hinge on their students' standardized test scores, may also be affected by the level of violence to which children are exposed in their community.[86]

Trauma and stress affect students' opportunities to learn and engage fully in classrooms and in school. Not all children who experience some form of traumatic stress are affected in the same way. However, students' experiences with trauma and stress often make it substantially more difficult for them to fully participate in their classrooms and schools. Children who experience traumatic stress are at increased risk of difficulty

---

78 Finkelhor et al. (2005); Duncan et al. (1994); McLoyd (1998); Gershoff et al. (2007); Rothstein (2004); Fryer & Levitt (2004).
79 Blodgett (2012).
80 Sharkey et al. (2014); Sharkey et al. (2012); Sharkey (2010).
81 Perfect et al. (2016); Bucker et al. (2012); Daud, Klintenberg, & Rydelius (2008); De Bellis Hooper, Spratty, & Wooley (2009); De Bellis et al. (2013); Kocosvska et al. (2012).

82 Sharkey et al. (2014); Sharkey et al. (2012); Sharkey (2010); Overstreet & Braun (1999); Schwartz & Gorman (2003); Henrich et al. (2004).
83 Perfect et al. (2016); Delaney-Black et al. (2000); Duplechain et al. (2008); Moradi et al. (1999); Schwartz & Gorman (2003).
84 Schartz & Gorman (2003).
85 Hinze-Pifer & Sartain (forthcoming); Bowen & Bowen (1999).
86 Sharkey et al. (2014).

processing and recalling information, engaging in expected classroom behavior, and learning. Students who experience chronic stress may struggle to consolidate memories, concentrate, pay sustained attention, and retain or recall information already learned.[87] Prior studies suggest that children who are exposed to community violence, specifically, may also suffer debilitating internal, psychological, and external behavioral disruptions. These internalizing or inward-facing psychological disruptions may include PTSD symptoms,[88] increased risk of depression, loss of interest in activities, feelings of worthlessness, changes in eating and sleeping patterns,[89] and increased self-criticism.[90] Children may also experience externalizing or outward-facing behavioral disruptions, including antisocial or aggressive behaviors and hyperactivity.[91] These symptoms can be triggered by circumstances that may seem to educators to be minor or even unrelated, or of which they are frequently unaware: loud noises, physical touch, aggressive authority figures, threatening gestures, changes in routine, or anniversaries of a traumatic event.[92] Absent concerted, constructive responses from educators, these psychological and behavioral disruptions can substantially reduce children's opportunities to engage and participate fully in their classrooms and schools, increase their risk for disciplinary exclusion (e.g., suspensions, expulsions), and diminish their opportunities to learn and succeed.

Educators' responses can aggravate or alleviate the symptoms of trauma. Teachers' understanding of, and responsiveness to, the ways in which children's experiences of their classrooms may be affected by previous or on-going trauma matter tremendously. Adults in schools, including both teachers and counselors, are often unaware of the degree to which children are exposed to traumatic experiences outside of school,[93] leaving them to construct incomplete and potentially inaccurate narratives about children's behavior and performance in school. Students' internalizing behaviors or externalizing disruptions can be easily misinterpreted by teachers as signs that students are unmotivated, don't care about their education, or lack respect for the teacher or their peers.

Misperceptions of student behavior, and the inaccurate narratives they support, are also influenced by implicit biases or stereotypes based on race, ethnicity and gender. Research in teacher preparation programs suggests that teacher training requires substantial, ongoing self-reflective work on how race, culture, and identity shape teachers' interactions with students as well as their instructional practice. All educators are unconsciously influenced by stereotypes in the larger society.[94] White people— predominantly women— comprise more than three-quarters of the teaching force in U.S. public schools. Research also suggests that teachers of color are affected by racialized stereotypes, both in their own identity development and in their interactions with children of color.[95] Stereotypes unconsciously shape how teachers interpret students' behaviors in ways that are harmful to their interactions with them.

Compounding the challenge facing educators, children who experience significant trauma are more likely to perceive their classrooms and schools as unsafe, and teachers and peers as untrustworthy or even threatening. Their feelings of insecurity and preoccupation with

87 Ford (2013); Perry (2000); Schore (2001); Wilson et al. (2010).

88 Perfect et al. (2016); Overstreet (2000); Boney-McCoy & Finkelhor (1995); Fitzpatrick & Bolidzar (1993); Horowitz et al. (1995); Kliewer et al. (1998); Overstreet et al. (1999); Lynch & Cicchetti (1998); Mazza & Reynolds (1999).

89 Overstreet (2000); American Psychiatric Association (1994); Durant et al. (1994); Farrell & Bruce (1997); Fitzpatrick (1993); Freeman, Mokros, & Poznanski (1993); Gorman-Smith & Tolan (1998); Lynch & Cicchetti (1998); Martinez & Richters (1993); Overstreet et al. (1999); Pastore et al. (1996); Howard et al. (2002); McGee (2003).

90 Da Fonseca et al. (2008); Frojd et al. (2008); Hysenbegasi et al. (2005); Puig-Antich et al. (1993); Reinherz et al. (1991); Busby, Lambert, & Ialongo (2013); Latzman & Swisher (2005); Pynoos et al. (1987).

91 Perfect et al. (2016); van der Kolk et al. (2005); Overstreet (2000); Durant et al. (1994); Farrell & Bruce (1997); Gorman-Smith & Tolan (1998); Hill et al. (1996); Lynch & Cicchetti (1998); Attar, Guerra, & Tolan (1994); Schwartz & Proctor (2000); Schwartz & Gorman (2003); Halliday-Boykins & Graham (2001); Purugganan et al. (2003); Lamers-Winkelman et al. (2012); Schwartz & Gorman (2003).

92 Keels (2018)

93 Guterman & Cameron (1999); Voisin (2007).

94 Kendi (2016).

95 Kohli (2008); Kolhi (2009).

personal security may increase risk that others' words and actions are misinterpreted as having hostile intent.[96] Educators' critical self-awareness and appreciation of how traumatic stress may affect children's experience of their classrooms are key to responding in supportive ways that enable all children to participate fully and succeed.

Inaccurate narratives about vulnerable children's motivation and behavior, particularly children of color, can influence educators' willingness to provide additional resources and academic supports.[97] Furthermore, traumatic experiences diminish how readily children trust others, creating a destructive cycle that can undermine the availability and quality of adult social support over time for children who most need support.[98] Adults with limited understanding of trauma may struggle to connect with students, increasing the odds of misunderstanding their needs or misinterpreting their behavior, and putting traumatized students at potentially increased risk of exclusionary discipline practices, including in- and out-of-school suspensions, as well as expulsions. Policies and practices that are not sensitive or responsive to trauma can lead to cycles of trauma in which students are victimized at home and then punished in school.[99]

This pattern is observable in the schooling experiences of children in Chicago with substantiated histories of abuse and neglect, who are much more likely to be suspended than other students, as are students living in neighborhoods with high poverty and crime rates.[100] This is of particular concern because of the strong evidence from other studies that students who experience exclusionary discipline in schools are at greater risk for a range of negative developmental outcomes, including lost instructional time, lower academic achievement, and increased likelihood of dropout.[101] While educators may believe that these types of punishments motivate behavior change, they can actually increase the probability that students will act out in the future.[102] In Chicago, intentional efforts to reduce the use of suspensions have brought about improvements in student safety, attendance, and test scores.[103]

The ways that educators interpret and respond to students' behavior influences students' subsequent engagement. Although many children who experience traumatic stress suffer difficulties in school as a result, there is also strong evidence that how adults respond to those children's needs can support substantial resilience.[104] Even in the face of seemingly far-reaching adversity, children have a remarkable capacity to adapt. Previous research strongly suggests that, to a substantial degree, children's capacity for resilience—their ability to cope effectively and demonstrate high levels of social and emotional competence while under high levels of stress[105]—is a function of their social environment, particularly their relationships with those around them. The stability of strong, supportive, and sustained relationships with adults in schools consistently predicts children's capacity for resilient behavior in the face of traumatic experience.[106] The school context can make a large difference in how trauma affects children's opportunities to engage and participate fully in their classrooms and schools. There is emerging evidence to suggest that schools with safer, more supportive climates can mitigate some of the direct negative effects of even the most extreme forms of traumatic experience.[107]

96   Cicchetti & Toth (1995); Margolin & Gordis (2000); Dodge et al. (1997); Lynch, (2003); Lynch & Cicchetti (2002).

97   Farrell & Bruce (1997); Gorman-Smith & Tolan (1998).

98   Overstreet (2000); Garbarino et al. (1992).

99   Crowder & South (2003); Bowen & Bowen (1999); Alva & de Los Reyes (1999).

100   Sartain, Allensworth, & Porter (2015).

101   Mittleman (2018); Skiba, Arredondo, & Williams (2014); Balfanz, Byrnes, & Fox (2014); Suh & Suh (2007); Christle, Jolivette, & Nelson (2005); Rafaelle & Mendez (2003); Muscott, Mann, & LeBrun (2008); Lewis et al. (2010); Rausch & Skiba (2004); Arcia (2006); Rocque (2010); Raffaele et al. (2002).

102   Skiba et al. (2002).

103   Hinze-Pifer & Sartain (2018).

104   Garmezy (1985, 1991, 1993); Richters & Martinez (1993).

105   Werner (1984); O'Donnell, Schwab-Stone, & Muyeed (2002).

106   Osher et al. (2018).

107   Recent research in Chicago (Hinze-Fifer & Sartain, forthcoming) suggests that high schools with safer, more supportive school climates may help mitigate the negative effects of localized exposure to homicide on students' attendance. Students who were exposed to a local homicide but attended a high school with a strong, supportive school climate were significantly more likely to attend school in the immediate aftermath. This was compared with students with similar exposure who attended high schools with weaker, less supportive or safe school climates, where attendance declined in the wake of exposure to a local homicide.

The availability and quality of social support from adult caregivers can help to moderate the relationship between exposure to community violence and negative emotional outcomes, including experiencing PTSD.[108] Children's perceptions of supportive relationships with adults can buffer them against the negative effects of excessive stress, and even increase their attachment to school.[109] This depends on educators' ability to understand, recognize, and respond to trauma.[110] Interventions to increase trauma awareness in schools have been found to reduce student aggression, out-of-school suspension, and the number of students diagnosed with disabilities such as Attention Deficit/ Hyperactivity Disorder and Oppositional Defiant Disorder.[111]

Besides being able to recognize the signs of stress and trauma, teachers need strategies for helping students cope with traumatic stressors to reduce their influence on learning and to produce a strong learning climate for all of the students in their classroom.

There are a number of preventative practices, as well as restorative discipline practices, that teachers can learn and employ. These can be supported by school-wide strategies and supports for students and teachers. Many schools have adopted Positive Behavioral Interventions and Supports, which emphasize teaching and rewarding positive behaviors, and doing so in a consistent way across the school. Many schools are using Restorative Justice in place of exclusionary disciplinary practices that ask students to take accountability for the harm they have done, build relationships, and problem-solve to prevent further problems. While each of these types of strategies take training, development, and practice, they provide support to individual students, and can promote a climate of trust and positive behavior in the school. Additional resources, like social workers, therapists, and wraparound mental health services may also be important supports to bolster the efforts of teachers to create a school-wide culture and practice that focuses on being aware of and meeting all children's needs.

---

108 Overstreet (2000).
109 Cohen & Wills (1985); Gottlieb (1991); Sandler et al. (1989); Ludwig & Warren (2009); Ozer & Weinstein (2004); O'Donnell, Schwab-Stone, & Muyeed (2002).
110 Overstreet et al. (2016); SAMHSA (2014).
111 Dorado et al. (2016); Walkley et al. (2013).

CHAPTER 5

Partnering with Families Supports Student Engagement

Engagement with families should not be viewed as peripheral or tangential to school improvement efforts. There is significant evidence that strong parent engagement practices are related to student achievement.[112] Students who have involved parents are more likely to earn higher grades and test scores, and enroll in higher-level classes; be promoted to the next grade level, pass their classes, and earn more credits; and attend school regularly.[113] Student achievement tends to be higher in schools where principals and teachers are open to parent engagement and view parents as partners in the learning process.[114] Further, there is a substantial body of evidence that parental involvement[115] influences the development of academic mindsets across multiple dimensions.[116]

Schools' approach to their relationship with families is evolving. Historically, parental engagement involved teachers telling parents information about their children and perhaps soliciting their support in specific ways. Now, parental engagement is far more complex. Engaging parents involves listening and appreciating their contributions and being responsive to the ways in which they would like to participate in the classroom or in the school.

Teachers understand that their relationships with families are critical to students' success and to the creation of a strong school community. In schools where there are strong relationships between school staff and families, students feel safer and more supported.[117] Much of what accounts for the large differences in safety among schools are the ways in which parents, teachers, and students work together and trust each other. Research in Chicago found that among schools that served students from similar neighborhoods—

with similar levels of poverty and similar levels of neighborhood crime—those that had strong relationships between teachers and families had much safer school climates with lower reports of crime and disorder.[118]

Teachers are more likely to remain at schools with strong family engagement. Schools that don't foster family engagement run the risk of having teachers feel less connected and potentially leaving. In schools where teachers and parents work together to support students, teachers are more likely to feel effective and continue to teach in that school from year-to-year. In a study of many different factors that might be related to whether teachers left or remained in their school, parent involvement was second only to school safety in importance for teacher stability, comparing schools serving similar populations of students.[119]

How can educators work together to create a school culture that prioritizes and supports family engagement?

Teachers Are the Primary Connection Point

Teacher-parent relationships where parent contributions and knowledge are valued can foster strong and trusting bonds. The teacher is the main connection that families have to the school. Families' experiences of school are deeply influenced by their experiences and relationships with their children's teachers. This makes the teacher-parent relationship critically important. There are many things for teachers to consider in determining how best to engage with families, including self-examining their existing practices. Approaching

---

112 Jeynes (2003, 2005, 2007); Bryk, Sebring, Allensworth, Luppescu, & Easton (2010).

113 Henderson & Mapp, (2002).

114 Gordon & Louis (2003).

115 Throughout this section, when we refer to "parental involvement" and "parents," this reflects what has been the primary focus of the research literature. We recognize, however, that

engagement of non-parental caretakers, including guardians and custodial caretakers, is also important for teachers and school leaders to consider in their professional practice.

116 Jeynes (2003).

117 Bryk et al. (2010).

118 Steinberg, Allensworth, & Johnson (2011).

119 Allensworth, Ponisciak, & Mazzeo (2009).

engagement of families through a similar lens as we have outlined with student engagement, we propose that the teacher sets the conditions that enable families to participate in ways that leverage their strengths and that the teacher's role is to be responsive in adapting their approach based on the needs and interests of their students' families. Moving from parent communication as a one-way, sporadic effort to a thoughtful, on-going, and mutually beneficial relationship can be an additional building block on the path to creating transformative learning opportunities for students.[120]

In schools where family engagement is a priority, the work of teachers is supported by principals who set organizational goals and strategies aimed at fostering a culture of family engagement. At the University of Chicago Charter School, the school leadership team was intentionally designed to build a culture of family engagement.[121] The three-person leadership team includes a Director of Family and Community Engagement (FCE), who, in collaboration with the school's full-time social worker, "attends to the facilitative, inclusive aspect of leadership, particularly engaging the parents and creating an environment that strengthens social and emotional factors that influence learning."[122] The FCE works closely with teachers and other school staff to cultivate and maintain a culture of continuous engagement with families. In practice, this means teachers make weekly calls to students' families, participate in drop-off and pick-up, and schedule informal meetings with families—all in service of providing multiple touchpoints and opportunities to build relationships, and help families feel informed and empowered in supporting their children's education.

120 Hassrick, Raudenbush, & Rosen (2017).
121 The UChicago Consortium and UChicago Charter School are both units of the University of Chicago Urban Education Institute.
122 Hassrick et al. (2017).
123 Hassrick et al. (2017).
124 Epstein (2009).

Principals Set the Tone for Their Schools

School leaders play a vital role in creating and sustaining authentic engagement with parents and community members. When principals and teacher leaders see parents as partners, they are better able to engage parents and community members in school improvement efforts.[125] The organization and culture of schools play a large role in the success of school- and teacher-led parent engagement efforts. Since there are many ways in which parents can be involved in their children's education, it is valuable for teachers and school leaders to work constructively with parents to determine what shared efforts can be most productive.[126] Principals can organize teachers around shared goals of family engagement and lead by example in their interactions with families. It is important for teachers and principals to think about how best to reach out meaningfully to parents to increase their connections. School leaders could engage staff in discussions of ways to involve parents in roles beyond the oftentimes surface-level tasks they are asked to participate in that are not related to their children's learning (such as bake sales). School staff may inadvertently marginalize families because they ask them to be involved in ways that do not reflect the crucial role they could otherwise play in support of their children's education.

Principals can support teachers' capacity to engage with families by providing professional development on parent engagement strategies.[127] Principals can provide resources to mitigate challenges, extra supports for students who are behind, and access to the resources in ways which support a culture of trust and support. They can also support teachers in accessing training and resources around understanding the influence that trauma has on student behaviors and experiences. As highlighted in the prior chapter, this knowledge helps support teachers in developing the trusting, supportive relationships with students that can help mitigate the negative consequences of adverse childhood experiences.

A Responsive Classroom Also Informs Family Engagement

Engagement strategies should be intentional and include strategies to reach parents who might face barriers to participation. Every parent wants the best for their child. Every parent wants to understand how their child is experiencing school and what their teachers are doing to foster learning and development of their

Principals Can Create a School Climate that Supports Family Engagement

- Schools that are welcoming to families set a positive foundation for engagement.

- A welcoming school office environment with friendly school staff who greet parents can create a climate of respect and openness.

- Schools can create easy opportunities for families to be involved and stay informed. School climate surveys are one mechanism which can provide principals with information about which aspects of school climate to prioritize.

- Strategies should be responsive to the ways in which families want to engage. There is no one-size-fits-all approach to engagement. Strong principals are reflective leaders who prioritize the needs of their individual school community when developing family engagement strategies.

- Communication with families works best when it is two-directional and when parent voice is visibly valued. School leaders and teachers can create a feedback loop with parents. This means frequent opportunities to regularly share important information, while simultaneously hearing and integrating parental perspective on both individual goals for their children's learning and development and on important school decisions.

125 Giles (2006); Louis (2003).
126 Epstein & Dauber (1991).
127 Weiss et al. (2005).

children. As teachers develop family engagement strategies, it is essential to reflect and think about the sorts of
opportunities they are creating for families to interact
with the teacher and the school. In many communities,
systems have been developed in ways which limit, if
not exclude, family involvement. Families can be shut
out of schools in obvious ways, such as a lack of school
communications in native languages. There are also
subtle practices that can make families feel excluded, for
example, receiving communications only when there is
a "problem" or something negative to share.[128] Parents
who have previously had positive experiences with
schooling or who have access to more social and financial
resources may be better positioned to engage in schools.
This can inadvertently perpetuate inequality of access
for families unless teachers and school leaders reflect
on the opportunities they are providing for engagement,
and how those are perceived by diverse parents. Many
schools in the U.S. today serve students from different
cultures and who speak a variety of languages at home.
Teachers and school leaders should review their engagement strategies to ensure that they are being intentional
about conducting outreach to embrace all members
of the school community and are effectively reaching
families who otherwise may face barriers to engagement.
This can include things such as reviewing and evaluating
school-home communication systems and structures,
parent-teacher meeting times and locations, school event
planning, and how well school norms and the physical
school environment reflects and embraces the cultures
and languages of its students and families. By taking an
active and intentional approach with a specific focus on
engaging parents who might face barriers to engagement,
teachers and school leaders can further strengthen
supports for all students.

It is important to put special emphasis on understanding the unique challenges facing families who
have different cultural backgrounds than their child's
teacher or the dominant culture of the school staff.
By understanding the power of culture in supporting
students' learning and development, teachers are
increasingly motivated to learn about the cultural backgrounds of their students and integrate this knowledge
into the learning opportunities they create in their classrooms.[129] Learning about family culture and background
can help foster connections in the classroom. As first
steps, this can include having literature that reflects and
includes characters with diverse backgrounds; high-
lighting historical contributions made by individuals
from multicultural backgrounds beyond those which are
already well known; identifying role models within fields
of study that reflect students' race and ethnicity; and
creating opportunities for students to share their cultural backgrounds in class projects and assignments.[130]
However, frameworks for culturally responsive teaching
also emphasize the importance of "deep culture," as educators come to understand different ways of viewing the
world or different conceptualizations of "the self" across
different cultures. These underlying aspects of culture
are critically important because they shape the ways
students learn and make meaning.[131] Concurrent with
providing a richer and more inclusive learning environment, teachers should also examine their own identities
and implicit biases. Reflecting on how the dominant
culture has influenced the development of structures
that perpetuate inequality can help foster understanding and empathy, as well as create the foundation for a
responsive classroom. This can be difficult and emotionally challenging work. School leaders can provide critical
leadership in supporting teachers to engage in understanding these deeper levels of cultural responsiveness
and in fostering a supportive and reflective environment
for adult learning.

Supporting a culturally responsive classroom
can help students in forming positive identities and
viewpoints of the world that reflect understanding and
appreciation for different cultural backgrounds. By
supporting students to appreciate and value diversity
and focusing on differences in culture as advantageous,
teachers can promote and recognize the unique and
valuable contributions their students' cultures bring to
the learning environment.

---

128 Evans (2011); Hargreaves (2001).
129 Gay (2010).

130 Kransoff (2016).
131 Fryberg & Markus (2007); Ginsberg (2015); Hammond (2014).

CHAPTER 6

School Leaders and Staff Co-Create the Climate for Student Success

It takes strong educators working together on creating supportive, trusting, and safe learning climates in schools to improve student learning. When teachers are left on their own to figure out how to create equitable learning environments in their classroom, the task can seem daunting, and their success will vary considerably.

> Without intentional, whole-school efforts to build strong collaborative relationships across the school community, individual teachers and student support personnel (e.g. counselors, social workers) lack support in addressing the challenges they encounter— leading schools to recreate the inequalities that exist in the larger society.

Thus, it is imperative for principals and other school leaders to critically examine the ways their schools are organized, including the systems and structures that they put in place and the quality of the relationships between and among adults, students, and families.

Taking a systems and equity perspective is essential because we know from research that everyone benefits when schools have a collaborative learning culture among all of the adults working in the school, including administrators, teachers, counselors, front-office staff, and security guards, and a culture in which all educators take responsibility for the whole school and are committed to creating a strong and inclusive climate. Principals, teachers, and student support personnel can work together on shared solutions to common goals, sharing leadership responsibilities so that all adults in the school work collectively on building and maintaining strong learning environments.[132] In fact, the way teachers and other staff work together in the school is more important than individual teacher qualifications.[133] Relational trust is key to successful collaboration so that all staff are able to work together on the factors that matter for success.[134]

To be able to work together successfully, teachers and school staff need to have a clear understanding of what they should be working toward and a means of measuring progress. This requires an ambitious, academically focused vision with clear goals around improving student attendance, grades, and behavior which can help steer teachers' work so that the collective effort is focused in the same direction. School goals must be clear, consistent, operationalized, and coherently aligned with the schools' vision. For example, a high school may set an ambitious vision of college enrollment and persistence for all students. This might require reexamining curriculum, for example, to make sure that it aligns with college readiness expectations. It may also require reworking the school schedule so that students are able to participate in college-focused seminars each year— tailored to their individual grade levels, for example. It also may involve reorganizing student support structures so that progress monitoring happens more regularly to identify students who are struggling. It may also require rethinking and reorganizing school-level structures so that students have consistent access to support networks that are opt-out rather than opt-in (e.g. mandatory tutoring sessions, whole-school study halls with pairs or groups of teachers working with students, lunchtime learning sessions, counseling sessions). Furthermore, it may also involve a more organized and targeted family engagement strategy focused on college-bound goals. This might involve providing caregivers college-focused information tailored to their children's grade level, GPA, and ACT scores and closely working with families to find a good college match.

---

132 Sebastian & Allensworth (2012); Sebastian, Allensworth, & Huang (2016).

133 Bryk et al. (2010); DeAngelis & Presley (2011).
134 Bryk et al. (2002).

Principals can support teachers in taking the lead with setting ambitious grade-level goals where, for example, each team of teachers is given the opportunity to provide feedback on the goal-setting of the other teacher teams. Teachers, in turn, could involve students in their own goal-setting process by helping them set personalized learning goals. To move goals forward, teachers and leaders should have a plan and processes in place for how to meet their ambitious goals and have data to evaluate how well their efforts are working. This requires that school teams meet regularly to examine student data and discuss whether or not movement has been made toward the goals. Teams can then work together to identify strategies and interventions. In order to do this kind of work, teachers and student support personnel must have protected time set aside each week to be able to meet regularly and teams should be coordinated and aligned so that there is a collective effort to work towards goals.

Principals can support teachers and other personnel by providing clear guidelines and expectations for collaborative team meetings, while giving teams considerable autonomy in how to move their work forward. Principals and teachers must also monitor progress towards reaching these goals and help teacher teams use data to drive instructional practice and improvement. This requires that school teams look at data at multiple levels, including student-, teacher-, department- or grade-, in addition to school-level data. Further, it is critical for principals to provide the necessary leadership to create a school climate and culture that prioritizes family engagement and supports teachers in their efforts to engage families. Many of the structures and expectations that support successful family engagement must be created and implemented at the school level. Communication is an important component of a school's plan for family engagement, involving both school-level structures and expectations, as well as responsibilities for teachers.[135]

Teachers and students need support to build their leadership capacity. By taking a systems-level approach focused on school climate, principals can support teach-ers to work together effectively. By developing structures to build teacher leadership capacity, principals empower teachers to take ownership over moving learning goals forward. For example, this includes involving teachers in school-wide decisions, purposefully distributing leadership responsibilities (as opposed to ad hoc task delegation) to teachers and other student support staff. Teachers also need their time protected so that they can work together purposefully and systematically on improving students' grades, attendance, and behavior. Finally, principals and teachers can work together to use data in effective ways to monitor progress towards goals and determine how effective current strategies are in improving student outcomes. This level of collaboration and shared leadership is not possible without a trusting, safe, and supportive learning environment conducive to organizational improvement and growth.

The most direct and impactful way principals can influence student learning is by building and maintaining a strong learning climate in their schools. As described in Chapter 5, in schools where staff and students report having positive school climates, students have higher academic achievement than in schools where staff and students report having weak school climates. What does it look and feel like for students who attend schools with strong learning climates? Students in schools with strong learning climates feel safe in and around their schools, so that they can focus their full attention on learning. They are supported by adults throughout school, so they can stay on track and automatically get help if they fall behind, and leaders consistently and clearly communicate their high expectations for both behavior and academic achievement.

As we mentioned in the beginning of this synthesis, the task of preparing students to meet new challenges and expectations requires not only a shift in the roles and responsibility of teachers, but also of school leaders. We now know that focusing on the school climate is not a "low-level" task for school leaders; it is the essential work for improving student achievement. Principals are the primary drivers of change in schools, but it takes strong teacher leaders to facilitate strong learning climates.

---

135 Leithwood & Riehl (2003).

Principals can serve as the bridge and the glue for the work that is happening across all classrooms. While teachers are working on instructional improvement and creating dynamic and engaging classrooms with high expectations and supportive learning climates, principals can support them by mentoring and providing meaningful professional development opportunities that are aligned with school goals. For principals, this means focusing on instructional leadership and organizational management tasks that align with a primary focus on climate.

Resources for Educators

Selected UChicago Consortium research discussed in this synthesis:

Teaching Adolescents to Become Learners: The Role of Noncognitive Factors in Shaping School Performance (2012)

Camille A. Farrington, Melissa Roderick, Elaine Allensworth, Jenny Nagaoka, Tasha Seneca Keyes, David W. Johnson, and Nicole O. Beechum

Summarizes the research on five categories of noncognitive factors that are related to academic performance, and examines whether there is substantial evidence that noncognitive factors matter for students' long-term success, clarifying how and why these factors matter, and determining if these factors are malleable and responsive to context.

Foundations of Young Adult Success: A Developmental Framework (2015)

Jenny Nagaoka, Camille A. Farrington, Stacy B. Ehrlich, and Ryan D. Heath; with David W. Johnson, Sarah Dickson, Ashley Cureton Turner, Ashley Mayo, and Kathleen Hayes

This research-backed framework illustrates how, where, and when the "key factors" to success develop from early childhood through young adulthood, emphasizing the kinds of experiences and supportive relationships that guide the positive development of these factors. It also emphasizes factors that are particularly malleable, as well as the age at which each of the key factors comes into prominence, offering adults the most promising window for positive intervention.

How Do Principals Influence Student Achievement? (2018)

Elaine M. Allensworth and Holly Hart

Principals are often seen as the primary agents of change to improve student achievement in their schools. Yet the role of the principal is complex, and there are many ways that principals might potentially influence classroom instruction and student learning. What matters most? Researchers used data from hundreds of schools to learn how principals were most effective at achieving higher learning gains on standardized tests. Then, they visited 12 schools, interviewing principals and teachers, to see firsthand what principals in schools with improving learning gains were doing that principals in schools without improving learning gains were not.

Supporting Social, Emotional, & Academic Development

Teachers, principals, and student support personnel all play an important role in creating a school culture that supports the development and success of all students.

What questions can the adults in a school ask themselves as they work to create a supportive school climate?

Teachers and Students

- Have I set up my classroom in ways that promote positive academic mindsets?
- Do all my students feel...?
  - ... they belong in this learning community.
  - ... they can succeed at this.
  - ... they will see their ability and competence grow with effort.
  - ... that the work has value for them.
- Am I using grade and attendance data to tell me who needs more support?

Principals and Families

- What can I do to develop a positive school culture in which students and families feel engaged and empowered?

Teachers and Families

- Am I establishing positive relationships with families at the beginning of the year?
- Am I communicating and engaging with families regularly so we can be partners in supporting students to succeed in class?

Principals and Teachers Working Together

- Are teachers working collaboratively on our common goals for students?
- Do we have strong monitoring and support systems for students that are opt-out, instead of opt-in? How are we assessing whether our systems and strategies are working and for whom?

All School Staff Working Together

- How can we create a culture where teachers, school staff, and families are working together in true partnership to support student learning and engagement?
- How are we allowing students' to bring facets of their lived experiences in to our school?

CHAPTER 7

Summary

Throughout this synthesis, we have focused on ideas that may seem low-stakes when considered individually, but when implemented in a cohesive, unified approach can fundamentally shift how students experience classrooms.

We have focused on insights from research that can support the creation of responsive, engaging schools and classrooms that advance educational equity. These ideas are framed within two complementary definitions of equity. First, that equitable schools and classrooms are places that enable everyone to participate fully in learning. This means that learning environments are developmentally appropriate and that staff are responsive to the needs, assets, and cultures of the specific children who inhabit those learning environments. It also means educators ensure that each child is afforded the necessary opportunities to thrive. This definition of equity requires that all of the adults in a school—principal, teachers, and student support staff—are working together to advance shared goals and have the appropriate training and resources to make that work successful. Second, equity refers to ultimate results. This recognizes the increasing emphasis in education policy to identify, understand, and reduce disparities in student performance across lines of race and opportunity, with the goal of achieving equitable outcomes for all students.

Creating student-centered learning environments, which promote and foster holistic development and focus on the leverage points which matter for improving student outcomes—engagement, classroom and school climate, understanding the influences of student experiences and the contributions families make, and responding to the diversity of a school community—may ultimately transform the approach teachers and principals take. This approach is rooted in the idea that the most effective way to improve outcomes for all students is not to focus on "fixing" or improving individual students, but to create a culture and a way of working together in schools that supports everyone's learning and development. This shift requires that both adults and students are engaging in developmental experiences and building strong, supportive, and sustained relationships. It means principals are guiding the school with a clear vision and empowering teachers to lead. Teachers are also then empowering students to take leadership in their learning. In this holistic approach, we see a the potential for a systems change in which these shifts in practice work in synergy to create a school culture that supports the success of all students.

References

Aceves, T.C., & Orosco, M.J. (2014)
Culturally responsive teaching. Gainesville, FL: University of Florida.

Allen, J., & Sconing, J. (2005)
Using ACT assessment scores to set benchmarks for college readiness (ACT Research Report Series 2005-3). Iowa City, IA: ACT.

Alspaugh, J.W. (1998)
Achievement loss associated with the transition to middle school and high school. *The Journal of Educational Research, 92*(1), 20-25.

Alva, S.A. & de los Reyes, R. (1999)
Psychosocial stress, internalized symptoms, and the academic achievement of Hispanic adolescents. *Journal of Adolescent Research, 14*(3), 343-358.

Allensworth, E., Correa, M., & Ponisciak, S. (2008)
From high school to the future: ACT preparation -- too much, too late. Chicago, IL: University of Chicago Consortium on Chicago School Research.

Allensworth, E., & Easton, J.Q. (2005)
The on-track indicator as a predictor of high school graduation. Chicago, IL: University of Chicago Consortium on Chicago School Research.

Allensworth, E., & Easton, J.Q. (2007)
What matters for staying on-track and graduating in Chicago Public Schools. Chicago, IL: University of Chicago Consortium on Chicago School Research.

Allensworth, E.M., Gwynne, J.A., Moore, P., & de la Torre, M. (2014)
Looking forward to high school and college: Middle grade indicators of readiness in Chicago Public Schools. Chicago, IL: University of Chicago Consortium on Chicago School Research.

Allensworth, E.M., Gwynne, J.A., Pareja, A.S., Sebastian, J., & Stevens, W.D. (2014)
Free to fail or on-track to college: Setting the stage for academic challenge: Classroom control and student support. Chicago, IL: University of Chicago Consortium on Chicago School Research.

Allensworth, E.M., & Hart, H. (2018)
How do principals influence student achievement? Chicago, IL: University of Chicago Consortium on School Research.

Allensworth, E., Nomi, T., Montgomery, N., & Lee, V.E. (2009)
College preparatory curriculum for all: Academic consequences of requiring algebra and English I for ninth graders in Chicago. *Educational Evaluation and Policy Analysis, 31*(4), 367-391.

Allensworth, E., Ponisciak, S., & Mazzeo, C. (2009)
The schools teachers leave: Teacher mobility in Chicago Public Schools. Chicago, IL: University of Chicago Consortium on Chicago School Research.

Appleton, J.J., Christenson, S.L., & Furlong, M.J. (2008)
Student engagement with school: Critical conceptual and methodological issues of the construct. *Psychology in the Schools, 45*(5), 369-386

Aronson, J. (2002)
Stereotype threat: Contending and coping with unnerving expectations. In J. Aronson (Ed.), *Improving academic achievement: Impact of psychological factors on education* (pp. 279-301). New York, NY: Academic Press.

Arcia, E. (2006)
Achievement and enrollment status of suspended students: Outcomes in a large, multicultural school district. *Education and Urban Society, 38*(3), 359-369.

Attar, B.K., Guerra, N.G., & Tolan, P.H. (1994)
Neighborhood disadvantage, stressful life events and adjustments in urban elementary-school children. *Journal of Clinical Child Psychology, 23*(4), 391-400.

Balfanz, R. (2011)
Back on track to graduate. *Educational Leadership, 68*(7), 54-58.

Balfanz, R., & Byrnes, V. (2013)
Meeting the challenge of combating chronic absenteeism. Baltimore, MD: Everyone Graduates Center at Johns Hopkins University School of Education.

Balfanz, R., Byrnes, V., & Fox, J.H. (2014)
Sent home and put off-track: The antecedents, disproportionalities, and consequences of being suspended in ninth grade. *Journal of Applied Research on Children: Informing Policy for Children at Risk, 5*(2), Article 13.

Balfanz, R., Herzog, L., & MacIver, D.J. (2007)
Preventing student disengagement and keeping students on the graduation path in urban middle-grades schools: Early identification and effective interventions. *Educational Psychologist, 42*(4), 223-235.

Baltimore Education Research Consortium (BERC). (2011)
Destination graduation: Sixth-grade early warning indicators for Baltimore City Schools: Their prevalence and impact. Baltimore, MD: BERC.

Blodgett, C. (2012)
Adopting ACES screening and assessment in child serving systems (Unpublished Manuscript). Spokane, WA: Area Health Education Center, Washington State University.

Bodrova, E., Germeroth, C., & Leong, D.J. (2013)
Play and self-regulation: Lessons from Vygotsky. *American Journal of Play, 6*(1), 111-123.

Boney-McCoy, S., & Finkelhor, D. (1995)
Psychosocial sequelae of violent victimization in a national youth sample. *Journal of Consulting and Clinical Psychology, 63*(5), 726-736.

Bowen, W.G., Chingos, M.M., & McPherson, M.S. (2009).
Crossing the finish line: Completing college at America's public universities. Princeton, NJ: Princeton University Press.

Bradshaw, C.P., Koth, C.W., Bevans, K.B., Ialongo, N., & Leaf, P.J. (2008)
The impact of school-wide positive behavioral interventions and supports (PBIS) on the organizational health of elementary schools. *School Psychology Quarterly, 23*(4), 462-473.

Bransford, J.D., Brown, A., & Cocking, R. (2000)
How people learn: Mind, brain, experience, and school. Washington, DC: National Research Council.

Bridgeland, J.M., Dilulio, J.J., & Morrison, K.B. (2006)
The silent epidemic: Perspectives of high school dropouts. Washington, DC: Civic Enterprises.

Brookhard, S.M. (2004)
Grading. Upper Saddle River, NJ: Pearson Education.

Brouwers, A., & Tomic, W. (2000)
A longitudinal study of teacher burnout and perceived self-efficacy in classroom management. *Teaching and Teacher Education, 16*(2), 239-253.

Bryk, A.S., Sebring, P.B., Allensworth, E., Luppescu, S., & Easton, J.Q. (2010)
Organizing schools for improvement: Lessons from Chicago. Chicago, IL: University of Chicago Press.

Bryk, A., Schneider, B., & Kochanik, J. (2002)
Relational trust: A core resource for school improvement. New York, NY: The Russell Sage Foundation.

Busby, D.R., Lambert, S.F. & Ialongo, N.S. (2013)
Psychological symptoms linking exposure to community violence and academic functioning in African American adolescents. *Journal of Youth Adolescence, 42*(2), 250-262.

Chang, H.N., Bauer, L., & Byrnes, V. (2018)
Data matters: Using chronic absence to accelerate action for student success. Baltimore, MD: Attendance Works and Everyone Graduates Center.

Center on the Developing Child at Harvard University. (2011)
Building the brain's "Air Traffic Control" system: How early experiences shape the development of executive function (Working Paper No. 11). Cambridge, MA: Harvard University.

Christle, C., Jolivette, K., & Nelson, M. (2005)
Breaking the school to prison pipeline: Identifying school risk and protective factors for youth delinquency. *Exceptionality*, Vol. 13, Issue 2: 69-88.

Cicchetti, D,. & Toth, S.L. (1995)
A developmental psychopathology perspective on child abuse and neglect. *Journal of the American Academy of Child & Adolescent Psychiatry, 34*(5), 541-565.

Clotfelter, C.T., Ladd, H.F., & Vigdor, J.L. (2015)
The aftermath of accelerating algebra evidence from district policy initiatives. *Journal of Human Resources, 50*(1), 159-188.

Cohen, S. & Wills, T.A. (1985)
Stress, social support, and the buffering hypothesis. *Psychological Bulletin, 98*(2), 310-357.

Cole, P.M., Armstrong, L.M., & Pemberton, C.K. (2010
The role of language in the development of emotion regulation. In S.D.C.M.A. Bell (Ed.), *Child development at the intersection of emotion and cognition* (pp. 59-77). Washington, DC: American Psychological Association.

Connor, J.O., & Pope, D.C. (2013)
Not just robo-students. Why full engagement matters and how schools can promote it. *Journal of Youth and Adolescence, 42*(9), 1426-1442.

Crowder, K. & South, S.J. (2003)
Neighborhood distress and school dropout: The variable significance of community context. *Social Science Research, 32*(4), 659-698.

Da Fonseca, D., Cury, F., Fakra, E., Rufo, M., Poinso, F., Bounoua, L., & Huguet, P. (2008)
Implicit theories of intelligence and IQ test performance in adolescents with Generalized Anxiety Disorder. *Behavior Research and Therapy, 46*(4), 529-536.

Darling-Hammond, L., Flook, L., Cook-Harvey, C., Barron, B.J., & Osher, D. (forthcoming)
Science of learning and development: Implications for educational practice. *Applied Developmental Science.*

Davis, M., Herzog, L., & Legters, N. (2013)
Organizing schools to address early warning indicators (EWIs): Common practices and challenges. *Journal Of Education For Students Placed At Risk, 18*(1), 84–100.

Dawes, N.P., & Larson, R. (2011)
How youth get engaged: Grounded-theory research on motivational development in organized youth programs. *Developmental Psychology, 47*(1), 259-269.

DeAngelis, K. J., & Presley, J. B. (2011)
Toward a more nuanced understanding of new teacher attrition. *Education and Urban Society, 43*(5), 598-626.

 References

Deci, E.L., & Ryan, R.M. (2008)
Self-determination theory: A macrotheory of human motivation, development, and health. *Canadian Psychology/ Psychologie Canadienne, 49*(3), 182–185.

Dodge, K.A., Lochman, J.E. Harnish, J.D., Bates, J.E., & Pettit, G.S. (1997)
Reactive and proactive aggressive in school children and psychiatrically impaired chronically assaultive youth. *Journal of Abnormal Psychology, 106*(1), 37-51.

Dorado, J.S., Martinez, M., McArthur, L.E., Leibovitz, T. (2016)
Healthy Environments and Response to Trauma in Schools (HEARTS): A whole-school, multi-level, prevention and intervention program for creating trauma-informed, safe and supportive schools. *School Mental Health, 8*(1), 163-176.

Durant, R.H., Cadenhead, C., Pendergrast, R.A., Slavens, G., & Linder, C.W. (1994)
Factors associated with the use of violence among urban Black adolescents. *American Journal of Public Health, 84*(4), 612-617.

Easton, J.Q, Johnson, E., & Sartain, L. (2017)
The predictive power of ninth-grade GPA. Chicago, IL: University of Chicago Consortium on School Research.

Eccles, J.S., Wigfield, A., & Schiefele, U. (1998)
Motivation to succeed. In N. Eisenberg (Ed.), *Social, emotional, and personality development handbook of child psychology (Vol. 3)* (pp. 1017-1096). New York, NY: Wiley.

Eccles, J.S., Lord, S., & Midgley, C. (1991)
What are we doing to early adolescents? The impact of educational contexts on early adolescents. *American Journal of Education, 99*(4), 521-542.

Ehrlich, S.B., Gwynne, J.A., Allensworth, E.M. (2018)
Pre-kindergarten attendance matters: Early chronic absence patterns and relationships to learning outcomes. *Early Childhood Research Quarterly, 44*(3), 136-151.

Epstein J.L. (2009)
School, family, and community partnerships: Your handbook for action (3rd Ed.). Thousand Oaks, CA: Corwin Press.

Epstein, J.L., & Dauber, S. L. (1991)
School programs and teacher practices of parent involvement in inner-city elementary and middle schools. *The Elementary School Journal, 91*(3), 289-305.

Evans, M.P. (2011)
Revisiting emotional geographies: Implications for family engagement and education policy in the United States. *Journal of Educational Change, 12*(2), 241-255.

Farrell, A., & Bruce, S. (1997)
Impact of exposure to community violence on violent behavior and emotional distress among urban adolescents. *Journal of Clinical Child Psychology, 26*(1), 2-14.

Farrington, C.A. (2014)
Failing at school: Lessons for redesigning urban high schools. New York, NY: Teachers College Press.

Farrington, C.A., Roderick, M., Allensworth, E., Nagaoka, J., Keyes, T.S., Johnson, D.W., & Beechum, N.O. (2012)
Teaching adolescents to become learners: The role of noncognitive factors in shaping school performance. Chicago, IL: University of Chicago Consortium on Chicago School Research.

Farrington, C.A., Porter, S., & Klugman, J. (forthcoming)
Do classroom environments matter for noncognitive aspects of student performance and students' course grades? (Working Paper). Chicago, IL: University of Chicago Consortium on School Research.

Ferlazzo, L. (2011)
Involvement or Engagement? *Educational Leadership, 68*(8), 10-14.

Fredricks, J.A., Blumenfeld, P.C., & Paris, A.H. (2004)
School engagement: Potential of the concept, state of the evidence. *Review of educational research, 74*(1), 59-109.

Fitzpatrick, K.M., & Boldizar, J.P. (1993)
The prevalence and consequences of exposure to violence among African-American youth. *Journal of the American Academy of Child & Adolescent Psychiatry, 32*(2), 424-430.

Freeman, L.N., Mokros, H., & Poznanski, E. (1993)
Violent events reported by normal urban school-aged children: Characteristics and depression correlates. *Journal of the American Academy of Child & Adolescent Psychiatry, 32*(2), 419-423.

Fröjd, S.A., Nissinen, E.S., Pelkonen, M.U.I., Marttunen, M.J., Koivisto, A.M., & Kaltiala-Heino, R. (2008)
Depression and school performance in middle adolescent boys and girls. *Journal of Adolescence, 31*(4), 485–498.

Fryberg, S.A., & Markus, H.R. (2007)
Cultural models of education in American Indian, Asian American and European American contexts. *Social Psychology of Education, 10*(2), 213-246.

Gay, G. (2010)
Culturally responsive teaching: Theory, research, and practice (2nd Ed.). New York, NY: Teachers College Press.

Garbarino, J., & Kostelny, K. (1992)
Child maltreatment as a community problem. *Child Abuse & Neglect, 16*(4), 455-464.

Garmezy, N. (1985)
Stress-resistant children: The search for protective factors. In J.E. Stevenson (Ed.), *Recent research in developmental psychopathology: Journal of Child Psychology and Psychiatry Book Supplement, 4*, 213-233.

Garmezy, N. (1991)
Resilience in children's adaptation to negative life events and stressed environments. *Pediatrics, 20*(9), 459–466.

Garmezy, N. (1993)
Children in poverty: Resilience despite risk. *Psychiatry: Interpersonal and Biological Processes, 56*(1), 127-136.

Geiser, S., & Santelices, M.V. (2007).
Validity of high-school grades in predicting student success beyond the freshman year: High-school record versus standardized tests as indicators or four-year college outcomes (Research & Occasional Paper Series: CSHE.6.07). Berkeley, CA: Center for Studies in Higher Education.

Giles, C. (2006)
Transformational leadership in challenging urban elementary schools: A role for parental involvement? *Leadership and Policy in Schools, 5*(3), 257-282.

Ginsberg, M.B. (2015)
Excited to learn: Motivation and culturally responsive teaching. Thousand Oaks, CA: Corwin Press.

Ginsburg, A., Jordan, P., & Chang, H. (2014)
Absences add up: How school attendance influences student success. Washington, DC: Attendance Works.

Ginsburg-Block, M.D., Rohrbeck, C.A., & Fantuzzo, J.W. (2006)
A meta-analytic review of social, self-concept, and behavioral outcomes of peer-assisted learning. *Journal of Educational Psychology, 98*(4), 732-749.

Gordon, M.F., & Louis, K.S. (2009)
Linking parent and community involvement with student achievement: Comparing principal and teacher perceptions of stakeholder influence. *American Journal of Education, 116*(1), 1-31.

Gorman-Smith, D., & Tolan, P. (1998)
The role of exposure to community violence and development problems among inner-city youth. *Development and Psychopathology, 10*(1), 101-116.

Gottlieb, G. (1991)
Experiential canalization of behavioral development: Theory. *Developmental Psychology, 27*(1), 4-13.

Grissom, J.A., Loeb, S., & Master, B. (2013)
Effective instructional time use for school leaders: Longitudinal evidence from observations of principals. *Educational Researcher, 42*(8), 433-444.

Guterman, N.B. & Cameron, M. (2010)
Young clients' exposure to community violence: How much do their therapists know? *American Journal of Orthopsychiatry, 69*(3), 382-391.

Gutgesell, M.E., & Payne, N. (2004)
Issues of adolescent psychological development in the 21st century. *Pediatrics in Review, 25*(3), 79-85.

Halliday-Boykins, C.A., & Graham, S. (2001)
At both ends of the gun: Testing the relationship between community violence exposure and youth violent behavior. *Journal of Abnormal Child Psychology, 29*(5), 383-402.

Halpern, R., Heckman, P.E., & Larson, R.W. (2013)
Realizing the potential of learning in middle adolescence. West Hills, CA: The Sally and Dick Roberts Coyote Foundation.

Halstead, J.M., & Taylor, M.J. (2000)
Learning and teaching about values: A review of recent research. *Cambridge Journal of Education, 30*(2), 169-202.

Hammond, Z. (2014)
Culturally responsive teaching and the brain: Promoting authentic engagement and rigor among culturally and linguistically diverse students. Thousand Oaks, CA: Corwin Press.

Hargreaves, A. (2001)
Emotional geographies of teaching. *Teachers College Record, 103*(6), 1056-1080.

Hassrick, E.M., Raudenbush, S.W., & Rosen, L. (2017)
The Ambitious Elementary School: Its Conception, Design, and Implications for Educational Equality. Chicago, IL: University of Chicago Press.

Hattie, J., & Gan, M. (2011)
Instruction based on feedback. In R.E. Mayer & P.A. Alexander (Eds.) *Handbook of research on learning and instruction* (pp. 249-271). New York, NY: Routledge.

Hazen, E., Schlozman, S., & Beresin, E. (2008)
Adolescent psychological development: A review. *Pediatrics in Review, 29*(5), 161-168.

Healey, K., Nagaoka, J., & Michelman, V. (2014)
The educational attainment of Chicago Public Schools students: A focus on four-year college degrees. Chicago, IL: University of Chicago Consortium on Chicago School Research.

Helms, J.E. (1995)
An update on Helms's White and people of color racial identity models. In J. G. Ponterotto, J.M. Casas, L.A. Suzuki, & C.M. Alexander (Eds.), *Handbook of multicultural counseling* (181-198). Thousand Oaks, CA: Sage.

Henderson, A.T., & Mapp, K.L. (2002)
A new wave of evidence: The impact of school, family, and community connections on student achievement. Austin, TX: National Center for Family & Community Connections with Schools: Southwest Educational Development Laboratory.

Hart Research Associates. (2018)
Fulfilling the American Dream: Liberal education and the future of work. Washington, DC: Association of American Colleges and Universities.

Hill, H.M. & Madhere, S. (1996)
Exposure to community violence and African American children: A multidimensional model of risks and resources. *Journal of Community Psychology, 24*(1), 26-43.

Hiss, W.C., & Franks, V.W. (2014)
Defining promise: Optional standardized testing policies in American college and university admissions. Arlington, VA: The National Association for College Admission Counseling.

Hinze-Pifer, R., & Sartain, L.S. (forthcoming)
The proximal impacts of community violence on students.

Horowitz, K., Weine, S., & Jekel, J. (1995)
PTSD symptoms in urban adolescent girls: Compounded community trauma. *Journal of the American Academy of Child & Adolescent Psychiatry, 34*(10), 1353-1361.

Horng, E., & Loeb, S. (2010)
New thinking about instructional leadership. *Phi Delta Kappan, 92*(3), 66-69.

Howard, D.E., Feigelman S., Li, X., Cross, S., & Rachuba, L. (2002)
The relationship among violence victimization, witnessing violence, and youth distress. *Journal of Adolescent Health. 31,* 455-462.

Hysenbegasi, A., Hass, S.L., & Rowland, C.R. (2005)
The impact of depression on the academic productivity of university students. *Journal of Mental Health Policy and Economics, 8*(3), 145-151.

Immordino-Yang, M.H. (2016)
Emotions, learning, and the brain: Exploring the educational implications of affective neuroscience. New York, NY: W.W. Norton & Co.

Immordino-Yang, M.H., Darling-Hammond, L., & Krone, C. (2018)
The brain basis for integrated social, emotional, and academic development: How emotions and social relationships drive learning. Washington, DC: Aspen Institute.

Ing, M. (2008)
Using informal classroom observations to improve instruction: Describing variability across schools (School Leadership Research Working Paper 08-1). Stanford, CA: Institute for Research on Education Policy and Practice.

Jeynes, W.H. (2007)
The relationship between parental involvement and urban secondary school student academic achievement: A meta-analysis. *Urban Education, 42*(1), 82-110.

Jeynes, W.H. (2003)
A meta-analysis: The effects of parental involvement on minority children's academic achievement. *Education & Urban Society, 35*(2), 202-218.

Jeynes, W.H. (2005)
A meta-analysis of the relation of parental involvement to urban elementary school student academic achievement. *Urban Education, 40*(3), 237-269.

Jiang, J.Y., & Sporte, S.E. (2016)
Teacher evaluation in Chicago: Differences in observation and value-added scores by teacher, student, and school characteristics. Chicago, IL: University of Chicago Consortium on School Research.

Kane, T., & Cantrell, S. (2010)
Learning about teaching: Initial findings from the measures of effective teaching project. Seattle, WA: MET Project Research Paper, Bill & Melinda Gates Foundation.

Kaplan, S., & Kaplan, R. (1982)
Cognition and environment: Functioning in an uncertain world. New York, NY: Praeger.

Keels, M. (2018)
Improving traumatized students' educational outcomes by shifting away from punitive and towards positive discipline: A toolkit for legislators, district administrators, principals, and educators. Chicago, IL: Trauma Responsive Educational Practices Project.

Kendi, I. (2016)
Stamped from the beginning: The definitive history of racist ideas in America. New York, NY: Nation Books.

Kliewer, W., Lepore, S.J., Oskin, D., & Johnson, P.D. (1998)
The role of social and cognitive processes in children's adjustment to community violence. *Journal of Consulting and Clinical Psychology, 66*(1), 199-209.

Kobrin, J.L., Patterson, B.F., Shaw, E.J., Mattern, K.D., & Barbuti, S.M. (2008)
Validity of the SAT® for predicting first-year college grade point average (Research Report No. 2008-5). New York, NY: College Board.

Kohli, R. (2008)
Breaking the cycle of racism in the classroom: Critical race reflections from future teachers of color. *Teacher Education Quarterly, 35*(4), 177-188.

Kohli, R. (2009)
Critical race reflections: Valuing the experiences of teachers of color in teacher education. *Race Ethnicity and Education, 12*(2), 235-251.

Koretz, D. (2017)
The testing charade: Pretending to make schools better. Chicago, IL: University of Chicago Press.

Kransoff, B. (2016)
Culturally responsive teaching: A guide to evidence based practices for teaching all students equitably. Portland, OR: Region X Equity Assistance Center at Education Northwest.

Kupersmidt, J.B., & Coie, J.D. (1990)
Preadolescent peer status, aggression, and school adjustment as predictors of externalizing problems in adolescence. *Child Development, 61*(5), 1350-1362.

Ladson-Billings, G. (2009)
The dreamkeepers: Successful teachers of African American students. San Francisco, CA: Jossey-Bass.

Lamers-Winkelman, F., Willemen, A.M., & Visser, M. (2012)
Adverse childhood experiences of referred children exposed to intimate partner violence: Consequences for their wellbeing. *Child Abuse & Neglect, 36*(2), 166-179.

Latzman, R.D, & Swisher, R.R. (2005)
The interactive relationship among adolescent violence, street violence, and depression. *Journal of Community Psychology, 33*(3), 355–371.

Leithwood, K.A., & Riehl, C. (2003)
What we know about successful school leadership.
Philadelphia, PA: Laboratory for Student Success,
Temple University.

Lewis, C.W., Butler, B.R., Bonner, F.A., & Joubert, M. (2010)
African American male discipline patterns and school
district responses' resulting impact on academic achievement: Implications for urban educators and policy makers.
Journal of African American Males in Education, 1(1), 7-25.

Louis, K. S. (2003)
Democratic schools, democratic communities: reflections
in an international context. *Leadership and Policy in Schools,
2*(2), 93-107.

Ludwig, K.A., & Warren, J.S. (2009)
Community violence, school-related protective factors,
and psychosocial outcomes in urban youth. *Psychology in
the Schools, 46*(10), 1061-1073.

Louis, K.S., Leithwood, K., Wahlstrom, K.L., Anderson,
S.E., Michlin, M., & Mascall, B. (2010)
*Learning from leadership: Investigating the links to im-
proved student learning.* St. Paul, MN: Center for Applied
Research and Educational Improvement/University
of Minnesota and Ontario Institute for Studies in
Education/University of Toronto.

Lynch, M., & Cicchetti, D. (1998)
An ecological-transactional analysis of children and contexts: The longitudinal interplay among child maltreatment, community violence, and children's symptomology.
Development and Psychopathology, 10(2), 739-759.

Lynch, M. (2003)
Consequences of children's exposure to community
violence. *Clinical Child and Family Psychology Review, 6*(4),
265-274.

Mahatmya, D., Lohman, B.J., Matjasko, J.L., & Farb, A.F. (2018)
Engagement across developmental periods. In S.L.
Christenson et al. (eds.), *Handbook of research on student
engagement* (pp. 45-63). New York, NY: Springer.

Margolin, G., & Gordis, E.B. (2000)
The effects of family and community violence on children.
Annual Review of Psychology, 51, 445-479.

Marks, H.M. (2000)
Student engagement in instructional activity: Patterns in
the elementary, middle, and high school years. *American
Educational Research Journal, 37*(1), 153-184.

Martinez, P., & Richters, J.E. (1993)
The NIMH Community Violence Project: II. Children's
distress symptoms associated with violence exposure.
Psychiatry: Interpersonal and Biological Processes, 56(1), 22-35.

Maslow, A.H. (1943)
A theory of human motivation. *Psychological Review,
50*(4), 370-396.

Mazza, J.J., & Reynolds, W.M. (1999)
Exposure to violence in young inner-city adolescents:
Relationships with suicidal ideation, depression, and
PTSD symptomatology. *Journal of Abnormal Child
Psychology, 27*(3), 203-213.

McGee, Z.T. (2003)
Community violence and adolescent development: An
examination of risk and protective factors among African-
American youth. *Journal of Contemporary Criminal
Justice, 19*(3), 293-314.

Mittleman, J. (2018)
*A school-to-prison pipeline? Exclusionary discipline and
the production of delinquency.* Retrieved from https://doi.
org/10.31235/osf.io/28qk4

Montgomery, N., Allensworth, E., & Correa, M. (2010)
*Passing through science: The effects of raising graduation
requirements in science on course-taking and academic
achievement in Chicago.* Chicago, IL: University of Chicago
Consortium on Chicago School Research.

Mueller, C.M., & Dweck, C.S. (1998)
Praise for intelligence can undermine children's motiva-
tion and performance. *Journal of Personality and Social
Psychology, 75*(1), 33–52.

Murphy, M.C., & Zerkel, S. (2015)
Race and belonging in school: How anticipated and experienced belonging affect choice, persistence, and performance. *Teachers College Record, 117*(12), 1-40.

Muscott, H.S., Mann, E.L., & LeBrun, M.R. (2008)
Positive behavioral interventions and supports in New
Hampshire: Effectives of large-scale implementation
of schoolwide positive behavior support on student
discipline and academic achievement. *Journal of Positive
Behavior Interventions, 10*(3), 190-205.

Nagaoka, J., Farrington, C.A., Ehrlich, S.B., Heath, R.D.,
Johnson, D.W., Dickson, S., Turner, A.C., Mayo, A., &
Hayes, K. (2015)
*Foundations for young adult success: A developmental
framework.* Chicago, IL: University of Chicago Consortium
on Chicago School Research.

Nansel, T.R., Overpeck, M., Pilla, R.S., Ruan, W.J., Simons-
Morton, B., & Scheidt, P. (2001)
Bullying behaviors among US youth: Prevalence and
association with psychosocial adjustment. *JAMA, 285*(16),
2094-2100.

Nasir, N.I.S., McLaughlin, M.W., & Jones, A. (2009)
What does it mean to be African American? Constructions
of race and academic identity in an urban public high
school. *American Educational Research Journal, 46*(1),
73-114.

National Research Council and Institute of Medicine. (2000)
*From neurons to neighborhoods: The science of early childhood
development.* Washington, DC: National Academy Press.

National Research Council and the Institute of Medicine. (2004)
Engaging schools: Fostering high school students' motivation to learn. Committee on Increasing High School Students' Engagement and Motivation to Learn. Board on Children, Youth, and Families, Division of Behavioral and Social Sciences and Education. Washington, DC: National Academies Press.

Neild, R.C., & Balfanz, R. (2006)
Unfulfilled promise: The dimensions and characteristics of Philadelphia's dropout crisis, 2000-05. Philadelphia, PA: Philadelphia Youth Transitions Collaborative.

Nomi, T., & Allensworth, E. (2009)
"Double-dose" algebra as an alternative strategy to remediation: Effects on students' academic outcomes. *Journal of Research on Educational Effectiveness, 2*(2), 111-148.

Nomi, T., & Allensworth, E. (2013)
Sorting and supporting: Why double-dose algebra led to better test scores but more course failures. *Educational Research Journal, 50*(4), 756-788.

O'Donnell, D.A., Schwab-Stone, M.E., & Muyweed, A.Z. (2002)
Multidimensional resilience in urban children exposed to community violence. *Child Development, 73*(4), 1265-1282.

Oldfather, P., & McLaughlin, H.J. (1993)
Gaining and losing voice: A longitudinal study of students' continuing impulse to learn across elementary middle level contexts. *Research in Middle Level Education, 17*(1), 1–25.

Osher, D., Cantor, P., Berg, J., Steyer, L., & Rose, T. (2018)
Drivers of human development: How relationships and context shape learning and development. *Applied Developmental Science*, DOI: 10.1080/10888691.2017.1398650

Osher, D. & Kendziora, K. (2010)
Building conditions for learning and healthy adolescent development: Strategic approaches, In B. Doll, W. Pfohl, & J. Yoon (Eds.) *Handbook of youth prevention science* (pp. 121-140). New York, NY: Rutledge.

Oyserman, D. (2008)
Possible selves: Identity-based motivation and school success. In H. Marsh, R.G. Craven, & D.M. McInerney (Eds.), *Self-processes, learning, and enabling human potential* (pp. 269-288). Charlotte, NC: Information Age Publishing.

Oyserman, D., & Fryberg, S. (2006)
The possible selves of diverse adolescents: Content and function across gender, race and national origin. In C. Dunkel & J. Kerpelman (Eds.), *Possible selves: Theory, research, and applications* (pp. 17-39). Hauppauge, NY: Nova Science Publishers.

Ozer, E.J, Weinstein, R.S. (2004)
Urban adolescents' exposure to community violence: The role of support, school safety, and social constraints in a school-based sample of boys and girls. *Journal of Clinical Child and Adolescent Psychology, 33*(3), 463–476.

Pastore, D.R., Fisher, M., & Friedman, S.B. (1996)
Violence and mental health problems among urban high school students. *Journal of Adolescent Health, 18*(5), 320-324.

Phinney, J.S. (1993)
A three-stage model of ethnic identity development in adolescence. In M.E. Bernal & G.P. Knight (Eds.), SUNY series, *United States Hispanic studies. Ethnic identity: Formation and transmission among Hispanics and other minorities* (pp. 61-79). Albany, NY: State University of New York Press.

Phinney, J.S., & Ong, A.D. (2007)
Conceptualization and measurement of ethnic identity: Current status and future directions. *Journal of Counseling Psychology, 54*(3), 271-281.

Puig-Anthich, J., Kaufman, J., Ryan, N.D., Williamson, D.E., Dahl, R.E., Lukens, E., & Nelson, B. (1993)
The psychosocial functioning and family environment of depressed adolescents. *Journal of the American Academy of Child & Adolescent Psychiatry, 32*(2), 244–253.

Purugganan, O.H., Stein, R.E., Silver, E.J., & Beneson, B.S. (2003)
Exposure to violence and psychosocial adjustment among urban school-aged children. *Journal of Developmental & Behavioral Pediatrics, 24*(6), 424-430.

Pynoos, R.S., Frederick, C., Nader, K., Arroyo, E., Steinberg, A., Eth, S., Nunez, F., & Fairbanks, L. (1987)
Life threat and posttraumatic stress in school-age children. *Archives of General Psychiatry, 44*(12), 1057–1063.

Quay, L., & Romero, C. (2015)
What we know about learning mindsets from scientific research. Oakland, CA: Mindset Scholars Network.

Rafaelle Mendez, L.M. (2003)
Predictors of suspension and negative school outcomes: A longitudinal investigation. *New Directions for Youth Development, 2003*(99), 17-33.

Rafaelle Mendez, L.M., Knoff, H.M., & Ferron, J.M. (2002)
School demographic variables and out-of-school suspension rates: A quantitative and qualitative analysis of a large, ethnically diverse school district. *Psychology in the Schools, 39*(3), 259-277.

Rausch, M.K., & Skiba, R.J. (2004)
Disproportionality in school discipline among minority students in Indiana: Description and Analysis. Bloomington, IN: Center for Evaluation and Education Policy.

Ready, D.D. (2010)
Socioeconomic disadvantage, school attendance, and early cognitive development: The differential effects of school exposure. *Sociology of Education, 83*(4), 271-286.

Reinherz, H.Z., Frost, A.K., & Pakiz, B. (1991)
Changing faces: Correlates of depressive symptoms in late adolescence. Family & Community Health: *The Journal of Health Promotion & Maintenance, 14*(1), 15-23.

Rocque, M. (2010)
Office discipline and student behavior: Does race matter? *American Journal of Education, 116*(4), 557-581.

Roderick, M., Nagaoka, J., Allensworth, E., Coca, V., Correa, M., & Stoker, G. (2006)
From high school to the future: A first look at Chicago Public Schools graduates' college enrollment, college preparation, and graduation from four-year colleges. Chicago, IL: University of Chicago Consortium on Chicago School Research.

Roehlkepartain, E.C., Pekel, K., Syvertsen, A.K., Sethi, J., Sullivan, T.K., & Scales, P.C. (2017)
Relationships first: Creating connections that help young people thrive. Minneapolis, MN: Search Institute.

Romero, C. (2015)
What we know about belonging from scientific research. Oakland, CA: Mindset Scholars Network.

Rosenkranz, T., de la Torre, M., Stevens, W.D., & Allensworth, E.M. (2014)
Free to fail or on-track to college: Why grades drop when students enter high school and what adults can do about it. Chicago, IL: University of Chicago Consortium on Chicago School Research.

Rothstein, J.M. (2004)
College performance predictions and the SAT. *Journal of Econometrics, 121*(1), 297-317.

Sandler, I.N., Miller, P., Short, J., & Wolchik, S.A. (1989)
Social support as a protective factor for children in stress. In D. Belle (Ed.), *Children's social networks and social supports* (pp. 277–307). Hoboken, NJ: John Wiley & Sons.

Sartain, L., Allensworth, E., & Portner, S. (2015)
Suspending Chicago's students: Differences in discipline practices across schools. Chicago, IL: University of Chicago Consortium on School Research.

Schwartz, D. & Proctor, L.J. (2000)
Community violence exposure and children's social adjustment in the school peer group: The mediating roles of emotion regulation and social cognition. *Journal of Consulting and Clinical Psychology, 68*(4), 670-683.

Schwartz, D. & Gorman, A.H. (2003)
Community violence exposure and children's academic functioning. *Journal of Educational Psychology, 95*(1), 163-173.

Sebastian, J., Allensworth, E., & Stevens, W.D. (2014)
The influence of school leadership on classroom participation: Examining configurations of organizational supports. *Teachers College Record, 116*(8), 1-36.

Sebastian, J., Huang, H., & Allensworth, E. (2016)
The role of teacher leadership in how principals influence classroom instruction and student learning. *American Journal of Education, 123*(1), 69-108.

Skiba, R.J., Arredondo, M.I., & Williams, N.T. (2014)
More than a metaphor: The contribution of exclusionary discipline to a school-to-prison pipeline. *Equity & Excellence in Education, 47*(4), 546-564.

Skiba, R.J., Michael, R.S., Nardo, A.C., & Peterson, R.L. (2002)
The color of discipline: sources of racial and gender disproportionality in school punishment. *The Urban Review, 34*(4), 317-342.

Spain, A.K., Ehrlich, S.B., Cowhy, J.R., Dasgupta, D.K., & Lockaby, T. (2018)
A community effort to support the transition from Pre-K to kindergarten. Chicago, IL: University of Chicago Consortium on School Research.

Sporte, S.E., Correa, M., Hart, H., & Wechsler, M.E. (2009)
High school reform in Chicago Public Schools: Instructional development systems. Chicago, IL: SRI International and the University of Chicago Consortium on Chicago School Research.

Steele, C.M. (1997)
A threat in the air: How stereotypes shape intellectual identity and performance. *American Psychologist, 52*(6), 613-629.

Steinberg, M.P., Allensworth, E., & Johnson, D.W. (2011)
Student and teacher safety in Chicago Public Schools: The roles of community context and school social organization. Chicago, IL: University of Chicago Consortium on Chicago School Research.

Steinberg, L., Brown, B., & Dornbush, S. (1996)
Beyond the classroom: Why school reform has failed and what parents need to do. New York, NY: Simon and Schuster.

Stipek, D. (2002)
Motivation to learn: Integrating theory and practice (4th Ed.). Boston, MA: Allyn and Bacon.

Suh, S., & Suh, J. (2007)
Risk factors and levels of risk for high school dropouts. *Professional School Counseling, 10*(3), 297-306.

U.S. Department of Education. (2018)
Chronic absenteeism in the nation's schools. Washington, DC: U.S. Department of Education.

van der Kolk, B.A., Roth, S., Pelcovitz, D., Sunday, S., & Spinazzola, J. (2005)
Disorders of extreme stress: The empirical foundation of a complex adaptation to trauma. *Journal of Traumatic Stress, 18*(5), 389-399.

Villegas, A., & Lucas, T. (2007)
Responding to changing demographics: The culturally responsive teacher. *Educational Leadership, 64*(6), 28-33.

Vincent, A. (2001)
Use of ethical dilemmas to contribute to the knowledge and behavior of high school students. *The High School Journal, 84*(4), 50-57.

Voisin, D.R. (2007)
The effects of family and community violence exposure among youth: Recommendations for practice and policy. *Journal of Social Work Education, 43*(1), 51-66.

Walkley, M., & Cox, T.L. (2013)
Building trauma-informed schools and communities. *Children & Schools, 35*(2), 123-126.

Werner, E.E. (1984)
Resilient children. *Young Children 40*(1), 68–72.

Weiss, H.B., Kreider, H., Lopez, M.E., Chatman, C.M. (Eds.). (2005)
Preparing educators to involve families. Thousand Oaks, CA: Sage Publications, Inc.

Whitehurst, G.J., Chingos, M.M., & Lindquist, K.M. (2014)
Evaluating teachers with classroom observations: Lessons learned in four districts. Washington, DC: Brown Center on Education Policy at Brookings.

Yeager, D.S., & Bundick, M.J. (2009)
The role of purposeful work goals in promoting meaning in life and in schoolwork during adolescence. *Journal of Adolescent Research, 24*(4), 423-452.

Yeager, D.S., Dahl, R.E., & Dweck, C.S. (2018)
Why interventions to influence adolescent behavior often fail but could succeed. *Perspectives on Psychological Science, 13*(1), 101-122.

Yeager, D.S., & Walton, G.M. (2011)
Social-psychological interventions in education: They're not magic. *Review of Educational Research, 81*(2), 267-301.

Zirkel, S. (2002)
Is there a place for me? Role models and academic identity among white students and students of color. *Teachers College Record, 104*(2), 357-376.

ABOUT THE AUTHORS

ELAINE M. ALLENSWORTH is the Lewis-Sebring Director of the UChicago Consortium, where she has conducted research on educational policy and practice for the last 20 years. She works with policymakers and practitioners to bridge research and practice, providing advice to researchers across the country about conducting research-practice partnerships, and serving on panels, policy commissions, and working groups at the local, state and national level. Her research on the factors that predict whether students will drop out of high school has shifted the conversation from factors that schools cannot control to factors that schools can influence; school districts across the country have adopt early warning indicator systems based on her Freshman OnTrack research. She has received a number of awards from the American Educational Research Association, including the Palmer O. Johnson award. She holds a PhD in Sociology from Michigan State University, and was once a high school Spanish and science teacher.

CAMILLE A. FARRINGTON is a Managing Director and Senior Research Associate at the UChicago Consortium. She is a national expert on academic mindsets and the measurement of psychosocial factors in academic settings. Her research focuses on understanding how learning environments provide opportunities for positive developmental experiences for students, how young people make sense of daily schooling experiences, and how school structures and teacher practices shape students' beliefs, behaviors, performance, and development. Her book, *Failing at School: Lessons for Redesigning Urban High Schools* (2014, Teachers College Press), outlines one approach to equitable school redesign. All of her work is informed by her fifteen years' experience as a public high school teacher.

MOLLY F. GORDON is a Research Scientist, Gordon conducts applied research that is relevant, meaningful, and timely for practitioners. She conducts qualitative and mixed-methods studies that are relevant for the local, state, and national education community and can be used to inform policy decisions. Her current research focuses on investigating how school leaders influence school climate and student learning, and on attendance policies and practices in pre-k. Gordon was previously a Research Associate at the Center for Applied Research and Educational Improvement at the University of Minnesota.

DAVID W. JOHNSON is a Senior Research Associate at the UChicago Consortium. His current research explores efforts to develop supports for educators that merge racial and cultural identity development and awareness with instructional improvement strategies. Other projects include research on understanding how exposure to community violence in Chicago affects school communities, with an emphasis on building the capacity of educators and schools to support and nurture all students. Johnson has also been closely involved in the planning and facilitation of a national network of school support organizations aimed at creating more equitable learning environments for historically marginalized and oppressed children and communities. His work reflects a thorough, ongoing commitment to building the capacity of public school educators to create developmentally rich learning experiences for all children, particularly across lines of racial, class, and cultural difference. Johnson is a former Washington, DC Public Schools teacher.

KYLIE KLEIN is the Director of Research Operations at the UChicago Consortium. She oversees research processes and procedures, as well as data security, contracts, and the 5Essentials survey. She supports the UChicago Consortium's research agenda development and strategic planning. Prior to joining the UChicago Consortium, she spent 10 years in district administration at the Chicago Public Schools (CPS). During her tenure with CPS, she held a variety of leadership roles in the Offices of Accountability and Special Education. While with the district she conducted several key applied research projects. She began her career as an elementary school teacher in Paterson, NJ as a Teach for America corps member. She is a member of the National Network of Research-Practice Partnerships (NNERPP) Steering Committee and a reviewer on the Museum of Science and Industry's IRB.

BRONWYN MCDANIEL is the Director of Outreach and Communication at the UChicago Consortium. In this role, she leads the UChicago Consortium's local and national engagement efforts. Currently, she is focused on strategies to make the Consortium's research more accessible to a broad audience. She serves as the organization's press liaison with local and national media. She oversees the communications staff, which produces research reports and manages UChicago Consortium's internal and external research review processes. She joined the UChicago Consortium after many years with City University of New York's division of school-college partnerships.

JENNY NAGAOKA is the Deputy Director of the UChicago Consortium, where she has conducted research for over 20 years. Her research interests focus on policy and practice in urban education reform, particularly using data to connect research and practice and examining the school environments and instructional practices that promote college readiness and success. She is the lead researcher on the To&Through Project, which provides research, data, and training on the milestones that matter most for college success. Nagaoka is the lead author of *Foundations for Young Adult Success: A Developmental Framework* (2015), which draws on research and practice evidence to build a coherent framework of the foundational factors for young adult success and investigates their development from early childhood through young adulthood and how they can be supported through developmental experiences and relationships.

9 780999 550922